✦✦

My Father's House

Philip B. Kunhardt, Jr.

My
Father's
House

RANDOM HOUSE | NEW YORK

9 8 7 6 5 4 3 2

FIRST EDITION

Copyright © 1958, 1967, 1970 by Philip B.
Kunhardt, Jr.

All rights reserved under International
and Pan-American Copyright
Conventions.
Published in the United States by
Random House, Inc., New York, and
simultaneously in Canada by Random
House of Canada Limited, Toronto.

Library of Congress Catalog Card
Number: 72–103976

Portions of this book first appeared
in *Esquire* and *Life* Magazine.

Manufactured in the United States of
America by The Book Press,
Brattleboro, Vt.

Contents

Prologue

THE DESK WAS NOT REALLY MEANT TO BE A DESK at all. It had originally been built as a table. Its four legs with their series of smoothly lathed bodies and necks had been hand-tooled sometime in the nineteenth century. What distinguished the piece was its cherry top, actually three planks of wood pegged and glued together to give the semblance of a single board. Over the years, two of the planks had begun to come apart with warp, leaving a tiny, straight fissure along the entire top. The wood of that top had a dark, rich grain to it, a couple of small knothole imperfections, and in the right-hand upper corner there was a large swirl from the trunk of the tree where it had been cut, leaving a tidepool of rippled, curved lines in an otherwise calm sea of straight grain.

The top of the desk had stains on it. They were dark black, inkish in look, made by man, not tree, and they had seeped into the grain, becoming part of the wood. The desk had three parallel drawers. They were made of pine, but on their fronts a quarter inch of cherry inlay had been added.

Bolted to that reddish fronting were hand-pounded, circular brass handles with simple face designs. The pine inside the drawers was old and dry. Some of the seams had lifted, occasionally allowing a bit of the contents to slip out and fall onto the rug below. There was dust in the drawers, along with the jam of paper, and there were cracks in the sides where a letter could get trapped and temporarily lost.

The desk sat against a ceiling-high bookcase on the wall of the back living room of an old house on a hill. Windows let the sun in for a few hours in the morning and for a short time in the late afternoon, and the slanting rays made the cherry of the desk top shine like bronze. At night a tall, thin table lamp with raised Chinese dragons coiled about its base cast a cold white light which turned the desk back to wood.

It was the desk of a man. Pipes and tobacco pouches always lay upon it, alongside a fishing reel or a jackknife or sometimes a thin gold pocket-watch. There were formal photographs in frames at the back of the desk. Two of them were taken by the same dignity-minded photographer—straight-backed, perfectly dressed, regally posed father and mother portraits. Another showed a bride in profile, dressed in her wedding veil and gown, holding a spray of lilies of the valley. In smaller, five-and-ten-cent-store frames, were snapshots of children. The main attraction of the desk was a heavy antique penny bank made out of a squatting metal Indian aiming a crossbow at a rearing grizzly bear. Pull back the bow, place the coin in the bow's notch, push the trigger and *clack!*—the bear got richer by a penny through a slot in his iron stomach. How many children, how many grandchildren, over the years, had received a coin from the delighted hand of the owner of the desk and shot it with glee, *kerplunk*, into that brown belly!

On the desk there was also a pair of long-bladed scissors and a sharp letter-opener, both housed in a single leather sheath. There was a yellow legal pad with lists of things to be done written on it. On a corner of the desk there was usually a current book, its nature obliterated by a handmade jacket of brown wrapping paper. There was a Bible in one of the drawers, a checkbook and piles of letters and papers. There was a solid gold pen and pencil, the wedding present from the bride in the portrait. It was obviously a well-used desk. It was cluttered.

Over the years, the desk had accumulated a wide array of possessions and papers. On the desk, and in it, was a record of a long passage of years. On it and in it were the letters, diaries, drawings, notebooks, photographs, files, messages of sentiment, the treasures, which, taken together, and blended with a son's memory, help build a picture of the father who was the desk's owner.

Heart Attack

January 5, 1969

I T IS SIX YEARS AGO TODAY THAT MY FATHER DIED OF A heart attack. He had been sick for several years, in and out of the hospital, in terrible pain at times, fighting against approaching death, doing mighty battle with the many things going wrong in the body which he had been so proud of for almost all of his sixty-two and one-half years. I was the last of his children to arrive at the hospital that morning his heart gave out. I was holding his hand, talking to him quietly, and he turned to me as if he needed something right away. Our eyes met only for a second that quick last time, and then he twisted his head and stared up at the ceiling of the hospital room. He gasped and his face began to swell and turn purple, and he seemed to be holding his breath, holding his breath, the way he always did when he was making a certain funny puffed-cheek face he called his "stubbill sparrow" face. Except this face never ended, the next breath never came.

Forty-eight days ago I had a heart attack. The pain had begun late the night before, as soon as I had got into bed.

All of a sudden, there was a thick, billowing ache in my chest and I got up quickly, without waking my wife, and began wandering through the dark house. I lurched from room to room. I began to sweat. I bent over the kitchen table, using my arms for support. I choked at the pain. I slid down on the tile of the kitchen floor and lay squeezed and groaning for what seemed hours. The pain muddied my mind, made it work in dizzy whirlpools. Again and again I thought of calling our doctor, but each time the notion seemed absurd. It couldn't be, it just couldn't be, I kept telling myself. I crawled on my hands and knees back to the living room and finally fell asleep in a straight-back chair by the fireplace. Morning would surely prove it all away. But morning did nothing of the kind.

At five o'clock I awoke. Now the deep, fierce pain in the left side of my chest reached its tentacles out toward my left shoulder and down into that arm and at the same time threaded its way up toward my throat and neck. The furnace in the cellar of our old barn of a house turned on, and I could hear the bright orange flare as the oil ignited. A few minutes later the big iron radiator pipes began to throb and clank and the radiator nozzles began to hiss. I looked about my living room, at the photographs of my five children which sit in a row on top of a bookcase, at the objects collected over the years which litter and ornament the tops and shelves of other bookcases, at the huge Oriental rug from the music room of the big house in Massachusetts where my father was born and grew up. I stood up and paced back and forth across that rug, cursing the pain, clutching at it with both hands, being half doubled over by it, wishing it away. After all, I was only forty years old and I had work to do and miles to go and this must be indigestion or heartburn— but I knew it was neither. Still my mind fought the realization and for a few hours more I would not admit it to myself.

I spent three days in the intensive-care ward of our hospital with instruments taped to my chest so that the beat of my heart was monitored every moment. After the first day there was no more pain. I lay in a narrow slot, one of a dozen open-ended cubicles that radiated out from a central glass-enclosed nurses' station. My wife was the only visitor I was allowed and she was limited to five minutes at a time. In and out Katharine came and went a dozen times each day, bringing me scraps of news from the world, of who had been called, how each of our children had been told about me, and how he or she had taken the news—bringing me herself. I would be lying on my back, staring at the green perforated ceiling of my cell, and the curtain would move, and there she would be once more. She touched me on the cheek and we looked straight and long into each other's eyes, showing each other our fear and our love.

I was not allowed to move, even to turn over. I watched the efficiency of the nurses as new cases were rolled in and worked over with fiercely kind and knowing hands. At night I thought a lot about the things I love in this world, and I thought about where I had come from and where I might be headed. My father drifted back into my mind over and over again. It was almost as if he were there and I was small again and we could talk. I was seeking truths, and they seemed, for reasons I was unable to fathom in those dim, floating hospital hours, to lie somewhere far back in my memories.

My heart attack had not been a bad one and by Thanksgiving I was in a private room. My children came to visit me. Fourteen was the age limit for visitors, so the oldest three had to sneak eleven-year-old Sandra up the fire stairs, and once in my room, she stood on the back rail of the bed to make herself look tall to the nurse. I waved to our three-year-old out the window, breaking all orders by getting out of bed and over to the window for the wave. She finally spied me up there among all that brick and glass on the third floor of the hospital, but she didn't seem too excited over the discovery and my sixteen-year-old son had to make her hand wave back. Over the phone she said to me each day, "You feel all right?" I would answer "Yes" and Sarah would tell me, "You come home." "I love you, Sa Sa," I said and I could hear her take the phone down from her face and say to her mother, "Daddy called me Sa-Sa. Daddy loves me."

Two weeks before Christmas I was home. My family shopped and saw friends while I puttered about the house, went through old papers and photographs, re-read old letters. At night I felt weak and fell asleep soon after the sun had gone down. But by two thirty or three o'clock in the morning, when the blood runs slowest and the dark and the quiet and the cold and the loneness come together, I was ready to get up. Each morning I watched dawn come, watched the black of the east turn to a blue-black, so that the invisible pine branches outside my study window suddenly became delicate dark tracings. A few looks later the east was silver and the needles of the pines were green again and the blood of the house was renewing its normal pulse and flow.

The last few days before Christmas everybody was out of the house, buying secret things and singing Christmas carols and having a skate on black ice, and I could sniff about alone, touching things that I had not touched for years, hitting keys on the piano for the reverberations only I could hear, opening drawers, sifting through boxes, looking through books I had not opened in years, reading a passage here, a poem there.

The seventeen years I have been a father have run by so fast, have been so crammed with work and play and adventure, that I have hardly thought about the fact of my own fatherhood at all. Yet I have kept files on all of my children, jamming the evidence of their existence and progress into folders and slipping them into a green metal cabinet in a hallway closet. Philip, 17; Peter, 16; Jean, 15; Sandra, 11; Sarah, 3. Now I had the time to take the folders out and read them through. Peter's file is typical of them. It begins with things he said when he was a child. "Tie this as tight as a stone," was one of his very early commands when he was telling us how to lace his shoes.

Once he asked me, "Daddy, what are you going to do when you don't live with us any more?"

"What's that?"

"When you go under the rock."

"Under what rock, Peter?"

"You know, under the rock and then up to God . . . Does God break us, Daddy? I mean, to make us babies again? Does He break us or does He squash us?"

There were letters Peter had written on Christmas Eve to Santa Claus over the years. "Dear Santa, we left our stockings in the front hall like last time. And we left some cookies in the living room. If you want to, write on the back." On the other side of the page, written in a strange hand: "Dear Peter, and all of you, the cookies were better in California. You left more milk in New Jersey. But I like this house best because the chimney is slippery. Love, Santa." And there were letters to the tooth fairy: "Dear Mrs. Tooth Fairy, yesterday I lost my first tooth. It was really loose in gym. I twisted it and it came out and the blood tasted really good. On the way back to my classroom, it dropped. It is lost. But will you please leave me the money prize anyway. Love, Peter." And on the back of this note, in much the same wrinkly, strange handwriting that Santa had used: "Dear Peter, thank you for your nice letter. I am sorry you lost your tooth but I am leaving twenty-five cents anyway. Do you remember when I left you the prize in California after you had your infected tooth pulled? Yes, I came through the window crack like smoke. I love you. The tooth fairy."

In the Peter file were his first drawings and report cards, letters, notes, a running account of his life so far, through jottings on pieces of paper. There was a mimeographed program of the lineups for the school football game which I watched him play when he was thirteen. Peter had made a touchdown, and as he ran back up the field with his teammates pounding him on the back, he shot a quick glance at me to make sure I'd seen. As soon as he caught my eye, I remember, he looked away.

In the Peter folder, too, was an English composition written a year ago, when he was fifteen.

"I've decided to write on a perfect father-son relationship," it had started, "because it's a subject of which I know. I believe that the most important thing in the bringing up of a young boy is his relationship with his father. His mother is, of course, equally as important but not in the eyes of the boy, for she is around him more, he takes her more or less for granted. His love for her is a different love from that for his father. I remember the nights when at quarter of eight we'd hear the sound of crunching gravel under a car's tires. Someone would shout 'Daddy's home!' and we'd all run to meet him at the door. I used to go out to the car and walk with him inside. Often I would walk to the end of the road and drive in with him. There was something about seeing him that made us all happy and excited, this sense never tired night after night, for I still go out to meet him.

"We used to have family football games in front of our house over the weekends. My mother, my brother and I would stand my two younger sisters and him, for he was the 'best.' His favorite play was when the older of my two sisters hiked the ball to the other, then Daddy would pick up 'the Bug,' as he calls her, and put her on his shoulders, then run for a touchdown. We were all too small to reach her for the tag. His team always won.

"A father should be a definitely dominant, majestic figure to his son, and at the same time a tender and loving person. I think that a good father should change as his son changes, like things his son likes, do things his son does. He should be able to treat his son as a man and also as 'his little boy.' He should not be always available like a mother, for this would destroy his brilliance. By going to work all day it makes the nights you see him much more important, and the weekends golden."

Recently I came upon a scrap of paper, a note my mother had written almost forty years ago. My sister had begun to wonder about death. The note said, "Nancy asked Dad about heaven and did people live again. Dad answered, 'Many think so, I don't honestly know.'" My mother had added to her note: "Everything you've said or done makes a difference in other people's lives, so that long after death you live in the world in a different form."

That is what this book is about—along with crunching gravel at the end of a day and golden weekends. Feelings shared, so different in their shapes, their shades, their sizes and their shadows. It is about a child's world and finally having to leave it. It is about the need to hold on to good memories during the dark. It is about stars and storms, about an old house upon a hill, about mountains and ocean, about a hero.

It is a book written to a father, from a son, with love.

✦•✦

The Hill and Beautiful Setting

AFTER MY FATHER DIED, MY MOTHER LIVED ON IN OUR house high on a hill in the New Jersey country, all alone for a few more years. Then it became too difficult for her to stay out there any longer and so she moved into New York City. Before the move there was the great accumulation of thirty-seven years of living and marriage and family to go through, all the letters and clothes and papers, her collections of antique toys and relics and photographs from the American past, her thousands of books, along with the possessions handed down from my father's family and from hers, all those personal treasures, each with its own magnetic pull, which made any act of casting-off one of agony. But the job had to be done and my mother struggled at it for six months.

No one had ever touched my father's desk since he was carried down those narrow front stairs and away to the hospital for the final time. His reading glasses still sat there, upside-down, one ear holder bent inward, as if he had placed them there yesterday. After two years his desk chair still sat askew, as if he had just finished writing a business note or another birthday letter, had pushed his chair away, risen and padded off to bed in his bare feet.

Now, when the move had to be made and the desk had to be cleared off and cleaned out, my mother silently nominated me for the task. I took the easy way out. I piled everything from the top of the desk and from the drawers into three cardboard boxes and two old leather suitcases and I drove them the hundred miles back to my house and put them in my cellar. There they have sat until now, being steamed by my furnace for four winters, growing musty in the dark damp of four summers, until finally on a frozen morning this December I was ready for them, carrying them upstairs one by one and stacking them in my study. In the early mornings I have sat on the floor of that little room and sifted through the contents of each suitcase, each box. Sometimes the memories have come too fast and strong together and have made me reel, made me shove everything aside for a while and get up and walk about the house, trying to unravel all those familiar sights and sounds and smells from so long ago. One suitcase contained nothing but photographs, dozens and dozens of them, lighting up for me different years, different moments and events in our lives. Another was filled with hundreds of notes written by my mother to my father that he had tucked away in corners of the drawers. "To my love, my grower of roses, may they bloom on our hillside for many happy years to come." She even wrote him every time they were apart for more than twenty-four hours. "The house seems very strange and evenings about 6:15 are very sad when there is no crunching step in the driveway, no peppermint eyes looking up the stairs at me. . ."

The desk had also contained countless notes and letters and cards and scribblings from his children and his children's children. Together they told him happy birthday for more than thirty birthdays, and they wished him Merry Christmas scores of times, and they asked him to get well or thanked him for a present or said happy valentine or some just said hi! A few of them tried to put into words what he meant to the writer. But they never caught the whole man, only a glint of him. Physical remembrances of times and places shared together dominated these letters, like this one written by my brother from college: "In just one brief word, I thank you so terribly much for everything, rather unsaid, that has been you—rides to the barn in the wheelbarrow, the high-hatted scull you once gave me, scuffing over the mountains and boat races at Zeeland Falls, a walk on a winter night over the hill to see the deer, early morning swims and turtle-flop, casting a fly on flat-rock pool at dusk, and everything that has said so much more than words can."

Another year, another birthday; this time word from my little sister at boarding school. "Dearest Dad, I can't wait to give you a *big* hug. How's the pool? And the garden? And the hill? . . ."

. . .

When I was a boy, back in those hothouse, prince days,
it was all running over a green hill; not a simple daisy hill, but
a heaping pine-and-maple shoulder which bouldered out of
a good Guernsey valley. Our house sat on the lap of the
hill—an old, high, well-squirreled, peeling white house
tucked in behind tall trees and got to by a labyrinth of rutted,
stony, hairpin roads, which years ago the delivery trucks had
learned to bypass and ignore. My mother had to drive the
three miles to town for everything, even special delivery.
That was all right by us, I mean my brother and my sister
and me; our hill was no place for trucks or for strangers. It
was a fact that hardly anybody ever knocked on our inac-
cessible green door, but when they did, you might have
wondered about the sanity inside, or rather the lack of it, so
much scurrying and peeping and preparing for the worst
took place before the door got answered. Then it was usually
some lost and dog-cowed man wanting directions to one of
the other three houses on the hill. My brother and I always
gave them to him with a lot of serious hand show, drawing
a map in the air, making the directions just as mazy as possible, so that he, poor man, trying to keep count of all the lefts
and rights on his fingers, would finally give up, throw the
fingers into the air and ask, "What kind of a place is this
anyway?" It was the same with the cleaning ladies. Fresh
from the civilized, benched rooms of their agencies, the poor,
gray, rheumatic things creaked out of our car, took one look

around, went *cluck cluck* to themselves with their dry chicken tongues, and quickly forced a promise from my mother to have them back in town before dark. And who could really blame them? For when night came, so did the brainless bats, darting, diving, flapping their witch-coat wings; so did the crickets, angrily tuning their deafening legs; so did the wind, tiptoeing through the Halloween woods, prowling the treetops, groaning the eaves of an old howl house; so did the foxes, barking their human, wounded, gooseflesh voices over the hill's blackness.

Our house had two floors and an attic topped by a peaked roof. A thick six-foot-high stand of boxwood and a screened-in porch obscured the main door and downstairs windows. From the front the look was open and east out across the valley, but from all other sides the house was hemmed in— monster maple and a few steeple pines to the north; horse chestnut to the south that dropped a heavy harvest carpet of shiny brown nuts in spiked green jackets each fall; tangled jungle of vines behind the house which took whacking and wading and hacking and beating to climb through to the invisible stone wall which bordered the gravel road hitching our house to the top of the hill.

The front door opened on a narrow hall and a thin, steep flight of stairs, banistered on one side, walled on the other. To the right of the door were the two living rooms, front and back. Duplicates in size, each was crowned by a circle of ornamental molding in the center of its ceiling. The front living room was used for sitting and talking, lying around, living. It had soft chairs and a puffy couch and a fireplace with a marble mantel, the dwelling place of three large iron candlestick holders in the shapes of flat cathedrals, their gilt spires surrounded by dangles of cut crystal which dappled the carpet with prism light when the sun hit them. Against one wall was an eighteenth-century roll-top maple desk with a cabinet top, in it thirteen panes of glass to recall the original states. On another wall the sober oil faces of our great-great grandparents on my father's side stared out of their cracked canvases, past their curliqued, gilded frames, their gaze hunting us out even in the furthest corners of the room. Sometimes, late at night, if we looked hard, our ancestors seemed to follow us with their eyes.

The back living room was the library of our house. It was jam-packed bookcases, all books from floor to ceiling—and my father's desk.

On the other side of the front hall was the dining room. Over a mahogany sideboard hung a large framed oil painting of fields and woods and a shepherd tending his flock at sunset —one of the few possessions my father had asked for and gotten when his father had died. The dining room table in the middle of the room was too low for my father, and he always banged it with his knees when he sat down to a meal. Then all the people at the table—my brother and sister, my mother and me—grabbed for our glasses to keep the water and the milk from spilling.

The pantry. A table where we children ate, except for Sunday dinner, until we were old enough to eat in the dining room all the time. A sink with a wood shelf and a window with a sill—the places where my father's winter plants sat, saucers underneath the pots to keep them from leaking after a morning's silver-pitcher watering. Glass cupboards with piles of china, stacks of crystal. A long shelf of serving dishes. A swinging windowed door to the kitchen, laundry room behind, and larder. This was Sophie's domain.

Sophie cooked for us for twenty years. She was tall, almost as tall as my father, with powerful arms and shoulders. There was no way to tell her age from her smooth brown features. The daughter of a Virginia slave and one of seventeen children, Sophie lived in a small room in the attic, came purring down the back stairs at six each morning and began making the house swim with the smells of cornbread and oatmeal and bacon and coffee. Of all of us Sophie loved my father best, waiting for his return home from business in the evening when he would always come into the kitchen to wish her good evening and ask about her day.

She liked to serve him, bending over with a silver dish and urging him to take more, smacking her lips and telling him he would need it for his health, all that running and chopping and work in the garden he did. Most of the time Sophie was kind and slow and serious, but once in awhile she didn't mind a good joke—like April Fool's morning when there was always something up at breakfast, salt in the sugar bowl, cotton in the popovers, boiled eggs with the egg

sucked out and water blown in—you could hear her chuck-
ling from the kitchen when one of her tricks worked. At
times Sophie would get fed up with my brother and me,
with our wild Kentucky Derbies through the kitchen, rob-
bing her cookie tins and leaving mud prints all over her
freshly scrubbed floor. Then she might grab at a knife from
the kitchen drawer to scare us. "Those boys!" she would
exclaim to my father with disgust. "They're just boys,
Sophie," he would say to her and smile, and that would seem
to fix it all up, she liked him so.

That was downstairs.

Upstairs there were three bedrooms. My mother and
father had one, my older sister the second, and my brother
and I shared the last. When our baby sister was born, my
father had two miniature bedrooms, practically closets, built
onto the back of the house over the kitchen. That's when
Lilly came, to be our nurse and to take care of the baby.

Until then, nobody had been able to put up with us. Nurses
came and went, practically never staying more than a week.
My sister and brother and I saw to that. My mother couldn't
cope any more with the hiring, so one day, at her wits end,
she sent my father off with instructions to go to a New York
employment agency and find the biggest, strongest, toughest
Scandinavian girl he could and hire her and bring her home
that very night, somebody who could really take care of all
our funny business. My father drove home that night and
Lilly stepped out of the car and was introduced all around

and shown her room. When she was out of earshot, my mother said, "I thought I told you big and young and strong. I thought I said Scandinavian." Lilly was under five feet tall and English and so thin and frail and middle-aged that it seemed to all of us this was some kind of joke, especially to my mother.

"I looked at all the big and strong and young ones," my father said, "and I didn't like any of them. None of them would fit in this family. And I was about to leave when I spied Lilly way down at the end of the bench and there was something about her face that made me know she'd like us, and when I told her all about us, she said she'd like to work here, so here she is, and isn't she wonderful?"

So it wasn't a joke at all. Lilly was the widow of an English sea captain. A net always held her mat of short, rippled white hair in place and her plain long face featured a high forehead, rimless glasses and a comical smile. Her shoulders sloped off sharply into spindly arms that turned even thinner at the wrists, but sprouted again into strong, claw-like, arthritic hands. In our house Lilly wore big-collared, short-sleeved cotton uniforms, light green or yellow, the skirts falling to her ankles, showing only the peep of two tiny laced boots. Whenever she went away on the train to visit her daughter, she wore dark, baggy affairs hidden by a brown wool coat with a heart-shaped extravaganza of squirrel fur about the neck. "Hello, Luv, I've missed you," was her inevitable greeting to us when she returned. Lilly ironed and mended our clothes, she mopped and made beds and cleaned our rings out of the bathtub and scratched our backs to sleep at night. She was too little and quiet to be mean to, and worked too hard for her size, so we helped her with the work, and when our new baby sister started speaking, she couldn't say Lilly, she said Yo-Yo instead. So Yo-Yo became her name and Yo-Yo stayed with us for over twenty years, too. The upstairs belonged to her, just as Sophie reigned over the downstairs.

Except for a couple of bathrooms, that was about all there was in our house—not counting, of course, the attic and cellar. They were both strange, dark, scary territory. Lonely, too—good places to go to cry. When feelings were hurt, when tantrums took over, when I had been caught in an embarrassment or just had been misunderstood; after scraped knees or overtired arguments or reprimands and punishments, the attic and the cellar were good places to lick wounds in, settle down again, start life over.

The attic was eaves, chests and trunks, dark shadows, looming shapes. Crawl to the very back of all that stuff and you were in witches' country. Shine a flashlight down the shaft that surrounded the thrust of brick chimney and spot way down at the bottom of the pit old broken bottles and white bones.

There was only one window in the main part of the attic and it was dwarfed by the peak of the roof. Its sill lay flush to the floor. You could lie there and get a good view of the tops of the trees, of the birds, of my father bending over his flowers far below in the garden. The window was stuck. Once I pried it open with a chisel. The little sill between window and screen was a burial ground for bees and hornets. For years they had entered through a rust hole in the wire mesh, couldn't find their way out and now lay in a brittle heap fed on by a black spider whose cloudy webs made the window practically opaque.

The cellar was even darker. The glare of the light bulb which hung from a rafter didn't seem to reach the corners at all. The walls of the cellar were made of earth. The steps down from the pantry were open wood planks. It was impossible to go down them without giving yourself away with a squeal of wood. Close to the steps was the preserve closet with its rows of paraffin-sealed glass jars of jams and jellies and the big gallon jugs of dark yellow honey my father got from his hives. Furnace, coal bin, woodpile, storeroom—that was the rest of the cellar. The dirt floor was always flooded by the spring thaws, turning the whole place to a dank dungeon for the summer. But in winter it was dry and hot from the incessant roaring furnace flame.

Waking up in winter stunned eyes, made specks of pupils, all that bright snow icing the hill. Blink! Rub eyes ready for seeing again. All that good big January snow covering up December's thin powder which had started to melt through and get gray. Blow a blast of hot breath onto the diamond glass, cloud it up, then thumb out binocular peepholes so that the white blaze outside can be taken in smaller doses. Now inch the window. Test the little freezing bar of air. Take courage—throw the window up completely. A wall of cold. Ears stay hot from the heat of the room, but everything up front—eyelids, nose, cheeks, lips—start to sting and buzz and tingle. Breathe in snow morning. Blow it out in a smoky stick that blossoms, hangs for a moment, evaporates in the crystal air.

Winter days on the hill were gloves soaked through from rolling snowballs, building forts, sledding hills, plowing our way through the heavy powder, breaking off icicles from the frozen, jammed gutters and eating them like cones. There were raw cheeks and runny noses and frozen toes and long winter underwear to be peeled off after a day's excursion. By mid-afternoon it was dark, but we stayed out anyway, tramping or skiing or finding someone to torment with a handful of snow down the back of his parka.

And then March came—and mud. And even though we hated to say good-by to the cold and the ice and the white, we began to pray for green and buds and hot sun again. And in April they came. Out of the winter-brown tarnished earth shot green shoots, and the trees of the hill turned live with buds, and in the fields we found the first daffodils and ran them home, screaming that spring was really here. We took off our shirts for the first time and felt the weak sun heat up our white backs and the days grew longer and the fires at night stopped and April turned to May. Rain fed the earth, the sun nourished it more, and everywhere there hung a feeling of expectancy, until finally it happened—the whole hill turned thick, lush, blinding green—and it was summer.

In the summer, our soft, winter-tissue feet got shod with elephant-hide calluses. By July not even a dagger rock, not even a trod-upon yellow jacket could do them harm as we ranged barefooted, our legs afire, over that green kingdom. In the summer, the hill was a menagerie of smells and growing things, of birch and spruce and prehistoric locust, of apple boughs and wild grapes, of goldenrod and a whole bouquet of other sneezing weeds, of sheep, and scythed or sickled hay, of milkweed and skunk cabbage and wild violets, of thick plastic sap drooling out of evergreen trunks, of honeysuckle and sumac and sassafras, of yellow grass dry as fire, of spongy moss muffling secret springs, of dust and clay and sun and salty sweat drying, crusting on sleek skin after a day's running.

The days were hot and sticky with steam. By July we were saying, "It can't get any hotter, not possibly, not by any reach of the imagination any hotter"—but it always did. Our attic turned into a Bessemer converter; open the door and the hot blast made you stagger. My father's suits, having commuted him to and from the city for his job of selling woolen goods, had to be hung on the line to dry at the end of a day. My mother tied handkerchiefs around her wrists to stem the tide down her arms when she was writing her Lincoln articles and children's books.

July, and then August. The heat months! Necklaces of glossy poison ivy dripped from the trees. Bees sucked at blossoms and soared off to their hives, their wings leaving behind a blur of dry dustpollen in the thick air. Grass grew an inch an hour. Even the trees prayed for a breeze. Relief would come if only their leaves could flutter and rustle a bit. Sluices of heat wrinkled off the pavement, off the car roof, off the garage, making dizzy liquid waves jump into the air. Birds drooped, sang softer. When my father came home from work, the tires of his car made the molten gravel crunch like soft crackers. The earth, dry as pepper, sighed for evening thunderstorms. Our dehydrated skin waited too. Finally the hot sky gathered together enough wet clouds to come crashing together in lightning streaks across the ragged evening, and then the waters came lashing, pimpling, hissing, drumming, flooding onto the thirsty earth. Those heat days finally put a stop to our running, and the search for cool and shade began. When rain did not bring it, we found it in the wet-walled, dungeon cellar of a deserted greenhouse. We found it in the damp, mulchy darkness of an empty silo. We found it in the igloo blackness of a rot-roof, out-of-use icehouse, and we lay on our backs there and slapped poultices of wet sawdust onto our hot chests, mustard plasters in reverse. If my mother ordered us out of our own pool fed by five Novocaine springs for waterlogging reasons, then we would head back into the deep woods, deep back onto the other side of the hill, where we swam again, this time in a leafy, stagnant, forbidden pond along with the water snakes and the skate bugs.

On those heavy, humming August evenings we ate dinner on the screened porch. We would get the water racing in a big pot on the kitchen stove and then we would go up to our vegetable garden in a field behind the house and pick three dozen ear of corn—six apiece for my mother and for us and an even dozen for my father—and we would run them back to the kitchen so they wouldn't lose their sugar, do a quick shucking and toss them into the steaming pot. Making typewriters out of our teeth, we ate the corn slathered with butter and salt and pepper. My father took the little blade of his gold penknife and slit the rows down the middle so that the meat would pop out when he bit and the skin of each kernel wouldn't get caught in his teeth. As we ate, the sky lost its glow, orange slipping into black. A breeze out of the north made the trees shiver; leaves brushed against the screen like soft fingers. Over the razz of the katydids we talked in hushed voices, planning a swim before bed, deciding who would sleep with my father on the porch. We lugged mattresses off our beds, led them down the steep stairs like elephants and threw them trumpeting onto the porch floor. Then we stepped outside, took off any little clothing we might be wearing, made skirts of towels and headed down through the garden to the long, twisting, stony path that went to the pool. My father led the way, and blindfolded by night, we could just make out the white heap he made ahead of us.

It was an old cement pool, built on a slant of the hill, surrounded by tall pines and shaped like an Indian's head. Down around the big curved chin was the shallow end. At the upper lip a constant spout of icy spring water tumbled out of a clay pipe which jutted from the cement wall a foot above the waterline. At the forehead there used to be a diving board before my father broke it trying for too high a swan. And at the crown was a yard-wide spill-dam that dropped the overflow eight feet down the back wall, making a brook that wandered the rest of the way down the hill. The far sides of the pool were rimmed with rocks; you had to do a balancing act to get across them. A few rocks beyond the spillway, an iron ladder slid down three steps into the deepest part. Each May we cleaned the pool, opening a great valve at the bottom of the back wall which let the brown, mulchy winter water spray out like a fire hydrant. As the water inched lower we would scrub the sides and bottom with heavy brushes the size of rakes which had sticks for bristles, loosening all the green slime and leaf mulch from the rough cement. It went on like that all day, scrubbing and whooping. In the last two hours you could not see through the water at all; it was like spinach soup, and at the end, because the emptying pipe was a little higher than the bottom of the pool, we had to make a funnel out of boards, somebody holding them up against the mouth of the pipe with his ankles and somebody else forcing the final spinach out with his broom. At the end, too, there was always a black snake down there to give us conniptions. Where was it? There! There! Around your ankle! Brooms became stilts, pogo sticks, pole vaults—anything to escape the snake. When the pool was clean, we'd let the cement bake out in the sun for a day, and then my father would close the valve and unplug the spring again, letting loose a great gush of crystal water as the pool started to fill itself for the summer.

In our night descent toes got stubbed by rocks along the path. When we finally arrived at the pool, we would drop our towels and just stand around for a while having a talk. My father would usually be first in. Suddenly he'd decide to go and he'd just leave us talking there, take a little run and arch out over the water. After the dive he'd swim underwater for maybe a minute, getting his blood good and cool for sleeping, then he'd finally poke his head out of the water like a seal, right at the spillway. He'd heave himself up on his arms and twist his body around so that he'd be sitting in the spill with his legs still in the water. My brother and I would follow, imitating his dive, staying under as long as we could until our temples throbbed with the cold, and then we'd surface, too, trying to act casual, almost lazy about the cold, and we'd pull ourselves up and sit on the dam beside him. Pretty soon our bottoms were pocked by the rough cement, but who could feel them through the numbness as everything from hindquarters down to toes whitened in that paralyzing water! We sat there and talked some more, and after awhile my father would slide in chest first, back curved like a shell—"turtle-flop" we called it—and then without a sound he would submerge and circle underwater for at least a minute. My brother and I strained our eyes to follow his course, but he was quickly lost in the blackened waters, and we would wonder, from our perches on the dam, in what new spot he would appear. It would usually be somewhere along the shallow end, close to the side for secrecy, the only evidence of the rise a widening ring where the water had been softly broken by his head and a deep, blowy breath, like a whale after a long sounding. Maybe a back dive for my brother and me off the dam now and a last, fast Tarzan swim across the pool. We hardly touched ourselves with our towels, we wanted to stay wet and shivering for going to sleep. Up the path we started again, up the three high steps my father had made of boulders, up through the honeysuckle, into the tunnel of arborvitae trees, onto the silken garden grass now, across the hobbling stone road, past the bird tray to our porch again. We threw ourselves on our mattresses. Fireflies flashed their specks of green, cold light outside the screen. Far off a dog barked. It was night, and now it was sleep, filled with peace and cool and amber.

.   .   .

I am talking now of an autumn morning when a door opened, the handle held in two fists so as not to let it squeak, and then one hand, big in the palm and thick through the fingers, came cupping at my woolen shoulder, shaking sleep from that shoulder with its gentle shaking, until my eyes opened off their soft pillow, and there was my father bending over me, grinning, holding up his finger to his mouth for quiet, saying, "I'm having a run now. Come!" That was all; but that was plenty.

For a moment then, after he had gone, I closed my eyes, tasting that last, lovely millisecond of sleep one hibernating moment longer. Then the blankets came off with an explosion; the yellow room was filled with arms and legs. Pajamas were Houdinied off, swapped faster than the eye for khaki shorts and a brown sweater smelling of wood smoke and belled at the cuffs from being rolled too often to the elbows. Feet shot into yesterday's damp socks like darning eggs and then into panting sneakers which got laced up to the ankles and double knotted there. Then I was off to take the stairs while touching only three of them and twist out the front door into morning.

There was my father spilling sunflower seeds from a tobacco can onto a shining ellipse of a tray, the aluminum of it getting pelted with each seed's dropping. That feed tray hung face high off the ground. It must have been the number-one restaurant for all the birds on the hill; you could see them clustering up the branches, waiting impatiently for my father's retreat. Four wires came off the tray like tent ribs, meeting at their apex a stronger, horizontal one strung between two colossal locusts which guarded our house like gateposts. At first when the tray was put there, cocksure squirrels got up speed along the trunks and flung themselves like drunk trapezists a good six feet through the air and onto the tray. Some skidded along the metal on their tense claws and fell over the rim, while others, more relaxed, made belly landings, filled their cheeks with seeds, and then, impassive to the wild police calls of the blue jays, used the tray for a swing. But my father had no sympathy for the squirrels. He called them robbers, whacked a Maginot line of nails up and down the wrinkled locust trunks, making dangerous propositions out of future take-offs. After that, the birds ate in peace.

Well, then it was time for the run. There was never any talk about keeping in shape; running wasn't for that. It was for the effort of it and for making that effort together. Off we started up the back road, walking at first, playing soccer with a small rock, dribbling the rock back and forth until one of us overpassed the other and lost it in the honeysuckle. Then I would jump onto the stone wall, prance along it like a tightrope walker, hop to make it harder, do it without hands, take four steps blindfolded and almost pitch over into the poison ivy at the fifth. After that there was a well to be shouted down, a drainage ditch across the road for testing broad jumps, and six crab apple trees to be shook and picked.

Our dog, an old pointer, gray at the muzzle and stiff in the hind legs, came with us. His name was Hundred, for that was the number of spots he was meant to have, although I never counted more than eighty-six, even with chalk to mark the counted ones. But who could imagine a dog named Eighty-six? "Here, Eighty-six! Come on, Eighty-six, boy! Where are you, Eighty-six?" No, Hundred was his right name no matter what his count. Hundred loped ahead to scare the deer. When we remembered to take him by the collar, make him go our pace, then we'd see scores of them eating breakfast all over the apple orchard. The does ate stupidly, munching the leaves like sheep, but there was always a buck about, ears pricked, eyes scanning, nose in a cold shiver, and when that buck got our wind, his tail shot up like a flag, wig-wagged a warning, and off the herd went into the brush like tan phantoms before our old Hundred, straining at his Adam's apple now, could strike a good point.

When we got to the beginning of the Ring Road, the serious business of running began. It was a woods road, no good for automobiles because great trees, humbled by ice, crashed down across it each winter. Except for the first quarter mile, nobody bothered cutting the trees out. The road circled the top of the hill. We always claimed it went an even mile from start to finish, until one Christmas there was a pedometer in the toe of my stocking, and then everything on the hill got measured. The Ring Road turned out to be a mile and a half.

In the fall, dead leaves piled up shin deep along the road.

and so the running there wasn't like most ordinary running at all. It was more a wading and a game of chance as well, for the next stride or the one after that might send you sailing, soaring, sprawling—tricked by a trench, tripped by a cleverly camouflaged branch. The leaves made a swishing, ocean noise as we channeled through them. Everything was bronze, Indian country. The sun was making white, molecular bars across our path which we broke and broke again like the beams of electric eyes. The sun was softening the frost, too, blooding up our ears, lighting the cobwebs silver which we breasted like tapes at the finish of a race.

Ahead of us partridge blustered up in blurred and whirring arrows, snouted out of their night nests by Hundred in the lead. Our breath shot out of our mouths in misty mushrooms, hung a moment and dissolved in the cellophane air. After the first wild burst of running we calmed to a jog, pumped our arms to get in the swing of it, peacocked our chests, hoisted our knees like show horses and searched about for likely Christmas trees with eyes that had a measure in them—nine feet was all our living room could take.

After a while the woods broke to the east, and we were running beside a fence at the top of the skiing field. It was a big, sloping field with hip-high grass. A dozen men with wicker brooms and twice that many small kibitzers burned it each November, and then, after the first blizzard, someone ran a tractor up to the top, backed it onto blocks and made a tow. People came from all around to ski there, and toboggan, although the next field down was a better field for that. If your brakeman dared to keep his foot up, you could shoot down twenty miles an hour, thirty after corn snow, aiming for the icehouse at the bottom, schuss right through the icehouse door and get stopped dead inside by the sawdust.

All at once, after the field, the Ring Road bent sharply round the hill away from the sun, and we dove into a dark tunnel of arching trees made darker still by the thick, octopusal wanderings of wild grapevines. It was cold in the tunnel, the leaves were brittle with frost. There you had to watch your step for turtles, toads and things with too many legs for comfort. Every fallen branch was a copperhead; you landed on one end and the other leapt up with a forked tongue and struck you in the leg.

It was in the tunnel that my father always pulled ahead. I watched his calves bulging with iron as his stride lengthened, and I worked my thin asparagus legs down to the stalks trying to keep up. I kneaded a stitch in my side, lagged, dragged behind. For new strength I pulled off my sweater and tied it around my middle by its sleeves. Then I set out to catch him. Now the running wasn't for show any more, or for feel; it was for keeps. It was numb running; nothing else mattered but to pass him. The gap closed. We left the tunnel behind and started the last stretch uphill. My knees buzzed like whanged funny bones. Hundy barked and leaped applause from the sidelines. My father breathed like a bull just ahead of me. And then with a last, vast, breathless sprint I took him at the pole, which was a giant branchless birch, white as an albino, there to mark the ring's fulfillment.

After that we walked home. The sun dried our sweat. We hardly talked at all. Finally there was my mother on the porch in a green wrapper, sipping a cup of steaming coffee. "You two have a good time together?" she called. And we nodded, came up the steps, laughed good morning, kissed good morning, and then we went into the house, my father in a great thrashing panic now about his train and I in a smaller one over my school bus.

It always snowed on the hill before Christmas. The first snow came out of a chill, chalk sky which hid the sun like frosted glass. It came easy in the beginning—big, and wet and smelling of ammonia. I remember one December we were playing football in front of the garage. The winter air made the punts ring. All of a sudden in the middle of a play somebody yelled, "It's snowing!" and then time was called without anybody calling it, and we stood there on the gravel catching the first lazy flakes on our tongues and faces. "It's really winter!" somebody said. My father blew on his hands and called for a huddle. He said it was to be a long despera-tion pass, desperation because he still had the storm windows to put on before dark. I leaned close to his ear and whispered, "Zombie," which was code language for a special play of ours. We lined up and signals were called. All down, set, signals one, two, three, four; and on five the ball cork-

screwed back through my brother's legs and I was digging
down the sidelines for the great forked maple at the corner
of our house. When I looked back over my shoulder, there
was the ball in the air, wobbling because my father couldn't
throw a perfect spiral, but a gigantic throw, a true despera-
tion throw, higher than the trees, lost for a moment in the
birch bark sky, now visible again, arching, falling through
the snow, missing the branches, bisecting the fork of the
trunk—as perfect a Zombie as ever got thrown. I leaped to
make the catch, although I really didn't have to. A great
hullabaloo followed. I was out of bounds! The touchdown
didn't count! The maple was unfair! What kind of rules did
we play by anyway? Smoke-mouthed players jumped and
bleated around my father for a decision. He only smiled. It
didn't matter. The snow was coming harder now, the sky
shaking it down like sieved flour. Everybody was putting on
leather jackets, zipping and buttoning and calling good night.
My brother and I went in to supper.

All that night the snow fell. You could hear it muffling up
the roof, making the trees creak, crackling the tinder jungle
of last summer's honeysuckle with its gentle cotton weight.
You could see it out the window making hunchbacks out of
the box bushes. With blinker hands and a cold, squashed
face you could watch the flakes fall and flash in the yellow
globs of tungsten light just outside the windowpanes. You
could crack a window, spoon up a handful of snow off the
sill and eat it. Then you could squeeze out a snowball, yell

"Think fast!" and toss it across the room at your brother.

After supper my father brought up wood from the cellar and built a fire. Snow came down the chimney and made the fire hiss. My brother and I lay on the brown rug and tossed square Chinese pellets under the big logs where the fire was white, and then the flames roared red and green and blue. My sister picked out a flat, four-fingered "First Noel" on the standup piano in the hall. My father said, "Tomorrow we'll cut our Christmas tree," and he began to move furniture about to make room for it. My mother made a chairback of her legs and gave us hair rubs, roiling up our hungry scalps with her strong fingers until our heads burned. Wind rattled the windows. My sister shivered in her knee socks. That was enough for my mother. She thrust the thermostat up to eighty-five. A minute later my father had it down to sixty-eight again where it belonged.

At nine o'clock chimes struck all over the first floor—the silver sliver of a bell from the mantel; the brass striking from the ship's clock on my father's desk; finally the cello tolling from the grandfather clock which stood like an up-ended coffin in the hall. The thermostat made a whir as the furnace got turned off for the night. Radiator pipes beat out a throbbing riff in the walls. My father placed the screen across the fireplace. All at once there was a wild dash up the stairs for the bathroom. My sister won. She locked herself in and turned on the taps. My brother and I waited: five minutes, ten minutes, a quarter of an hour. We slipped notes written in blood underneath the door which threatened burial alive if she didn't open up. My brother said, "What a good skeleton key!" in a loud voice, and he rattled a jack-knife blade in the lock. Finally the door opened and through the steam there was an angry clown smocked in blue flannel down to the ankles, brown hair bagged and wagging in a shapeless snood, face blotched with calamine and other caking lotions. We screamed insults, sang "Here Comes the Bride," made trampolines of our beds and then dove underneath them to escape the wild howling howitzer haymakers flung at us by our fiercely fisted, marvelous hell-and-scissors sister.

In the brown warmth of an old snowhouse three children fought at a private, scrambling incubator war. To them old age was rings on a tree or moldy freckles on a bald head. To them courage was a prince with a silver shield; pity was tears for a broken wing; torture was a bellyache from a green apple; hate was the venom felt for the sleazy huntsman who left a three-legged doe to stilt and bleed and wobble through the snow woods; graves were for pollywogs found floating one morning in a fish bowl, the promise of a frog poking out of the gray oyster wads like horns; God was a "Now I lay me" old man who watched over all living things; war was a parade; laughing was April Fool's when Sophie stuffed pop-overs with cotton and served them for breakfast; the new sister swelling the mother's stomach must have been swallowed. To them life was a season, now hot now luke now cold, now night with foxes barking under the sprinkled stars, now thunder, now mud, now morning. Life was an old wood house on an everyday new hill.

In the middle of our battle my father came into the room with *The Christmas Carol* underneath his arm. He said, "Quiet! Everybody quiet and straight into bed," or he wouldn't read. Then we were quiet, sliding down between our glacier sheets, my brother and I in one room, my sister in the next. My father opened the door between them, set a chair there and began to read. His voice was so deep, so full of ghosts and of blizzards and of Christmas, we writhed, twisted in our beds, drew ourselves up like turtles, stretched flat again like flounders, and fought sleep. But before the chapter was through my head was a dizzy ton on the pillow. And then I could hardly hear the *clop* of the book as it was closed or the window being inched or the snow-howl over the sheeted hill, could hardly feel at all the tender touching of that giant gentle hand good night.

His Country

I N THE 1940'S DURING THE WAR, THE GREATEST ENTER-
tainment our family had was a slide evening. We
would move the horsehair couch away from its normal
home against a wall of the front living room where it sat
beneath the gilt-framed oil portraits of our great-great German grandparents, and that pale-green wall would become
the screen. My father would meticulously set up the slide
projector on a little table in front of the fireplace and snap
on the high-powered light and cooling blower. He would
fool around with the focus, getting any hairs out from inside the machine that might be enlarged to the size of ropes
on the wall. Then he would place all the boxes of slides he
planned to show us that night in a pile beside him where he
could fumble for them when they were needed. The slides
had to be fed one by one into that primitive machine, each
pushing its predecessor out of the way on a narrow track,
and the slide had to be retrieved immediately after each
projection. Before inserting a slide my father had to hold up
each one to the glow of the projector and sight through it to

make sure the picture was upside down and backwards so it would come out right-side up and frontwards on the wall.

In the late 1930's my father had bought a miniature German camera and begun to photograph the hill in color during all its seasons. He photographed holidays, too, and special family events and gatherings, and he always took his camera on our summer vacations so we would have a record of the part of the northeast he had picked for us to live in and explore each August. My father never would have thought of going out West, to ranch country, or to the High Sierras or to Canada lakes. He stuck to places he had been introduced to and fallen in love with when he was young, or places where friends or family went, to New England mostly, but it had to be wild country to qualify, it had to be large country, it had to present a challenge.

The flat yellow Kodak boxes of developed color film grew in number over the years until a whole shelf in my father's pipe and tool closet in the downstairs hall was packed with them, each box marked in his careful, rolling script with the date and the place and the names of the people in the pictures inside.

On slide nights, as the audience gathered and made a circle of chairs or pillows on the floor, there was always a lot of yelling for someone's favorite box—"the big storm" or "let's see Maine" or "the White Mountains." Sometimes it was "the Adirondacks" or "Lake George" or "Isle au Haut"—or just scenes from the hill, the pool and the deer and the house and the view from our front steps that my father took a hundred different times, at dawns, at dusks, after snow and ice, during rain and rainbow. Each time that scene was taken the color slide showed the bird feed tray in the foreground and my father's garden stretching downhill to the white marble bench, and then the jungle of treetops and far below the valley, stretching to the horizon—the scene in spring green, in mists, in cloaks of snow, beneath scowling skies, under tapestries of autumn colors.

Everybody was assembled and the lights extinguished and the show would start. Then there would be catching of breaths or cries or sighs when a long-forgotten beauty suddenly flashed upon our wall. We'd tell my father to hold it there, we wanted to study it, and he left the scene shining on the green wall for a while, but never too long, for he told us that even with the blower, the emulsions on the film might start to melt after fifteen seconds. We would call out side memories to each other, and laugh and hoot at a dress of my sister's that was out of style now, and when someone wanted to point out something special in a picture, he would crawl right up to the wall on his stomach and reach up and put his finger on the person or dog or mountain peak he wanted to say something about.

When my father finally switched off the projector, everyone clapped. Even though the show was over and we were back in our own living room again, and the lights were on and sleep was being suggested by my mother who could

spot a yawn a mile away, still the talk of the pictures continued, each of us choosing his favorites of the night, or
commenting on the color of a July evening's sky that no one
could believe had ever been that red.

When I was moved out of the intensive-care ward and
into a room with a telephone, my brother called from Boston
to say he was coming to visit me in the hospital and what
could he bring. I asked him to bring Dad's slides. They were
practically the only things Ken had taken away from our
house on the hill after our father's death. Now I needed
them, to share again those scenes, to feel close to their taker.

I was sitting up in bed, staring out the hospital window
at the new day, when my brother pushed open the door to
my room, poked his head in, saw it was really me, and appeared fully, carrying the case of slides. "Thank God you're
alive, Bro," he said, taking me by the shoulder and giving
me a shake.

For an hour or so we went through the boxes of slides.
Ken had put them in some kind of order, and now with great
care he showed me the different categories, arranged by
years and places. The conversation went slowly; neither of
us was anxious to say too much. Each knew that the case
contained a last look at our beginnings and our roots, our
early adventures as seen through the eyes of our common
father. We looked at each other differently than we ever
had done before, as in the waning winter afternoon we shook

hands good-by, and then he was gone with "Take care, Bro. We need you."

My son Peter brought me my newfangled slide projector from home, and now the two of us began to fill its carousels which hold eighty pictures apiece. Peter worked swiftly, loading the carousels as if he were dealing cards, slipping the slides in backwards and upside down—1968 newfangledness hadn't gone as far as to correct that yet—and when it was dark outside, we placed the projector on the table that swung across my bed, set a carousel in place and snapped on the bright lamp. A rectangular block of white light leaped out upon the wall of the hospital room. I pressed the projector release button, the carousel turned, a slide dropped into place behind the lens, I focused, and there, in an instant, thirty years were wiped away and the father of my youth was smiling back at me from the wall. Someone, perhaps my mother, perhaps I, had taken the camera away from him —a rare occurrence in itself—and made him stand still for a shot. His face was square and large, with wide-set eyes and a shock of dark hair across his broad forehead. The smile seemed to consume the face, seemed to be him, rather than part of him. It did not end at the eyes which sparked with mirth, nor with the crow's-foot crinkles that spread from the side of either eye, nor with the flared nostrils in that solid nose, nor with the tongue that darted from that slightly open, upturned mouth. The smile seemed rather to continue over the whole huge frame of the man, into his powerful shoulders and body, even into his hands. The background of the picture was nondescript; I could not tell whether it was hill or mountain or sea country. But by that smile, so relaxed, so outgoing, so filled with pride and vigor and warmth, I could tell he was somewhere in his country.

For hours I watched those slides that first afternoon, and I continued to project and study and take delight in all those images out of my past for the next few days. They helped create a special picture of my father—my gossamer memories suddenly given vivid shape and form and color. After watching the slides, something of my father seemed alive again in me, something of his need for big land, his love of the wild, the recuperative powers of physical exertion.

He hated with a passion cities, pavement, signboards—any foolish thing that man had done that got in the way of how the world was made in the first place. He absolutely refused to stay in the city where he worked overnight, saying he couldn't breathe in there, he needed the clear air of the hill. His country was ponds and lakes and rushing streams and waterfalls and mountains. The mountains we traveled to in his short summer vacations were spired kingdoms to him, and we climbed them, through the thick trees at the base, pumping away as the trees grew shorter, finally breaking tree line, on the base rock now, up pinnacles and cones of rock, stopping every once in a while to throw off our back packs and pant and moan and slap water on our faces from a brook in a crevasse or a summit lake, my brother and I almost dying of exhaustion, and my father waiting for us to get back up, lighting his pipe, never seeming to need a rest at all, not even out of breath, not even puffing.

His country was vast ranges of mountains, of dawn making a jagged black line out of distant peaks; of a white lake of tufted clouds floating below us as we stood lords of a summit; of a streak of wind-whipped rain racing over the shine of an icy mountain lake; of mist-wrapped mountainsides; of cold blue days when the wind took the few white cloud balls over the mountains like missiles, making the cloud shadows race over the peaks, sudden fleeting eclipses of silver.

This country was the Adirondacks, the "cloud-splitter" Mount Marcy, McIntyre, Whiteface, Giant. Or it was the White Mountains, the Presidential Range—Jefferson, Adams, Washington, Lincoln. By taking us there and teaching us how to climb and making us feel our calves and thighs fill up with agony on a steep trail and pack straps cut into our shoulders and breath come short, and how to wait for our second wind, and by showing us the thrill of reaching a summit, he made his country our country forevermore.

In the White Mountains it was Lafayette, too, and Zeeland Falls where mountain water came down the black boulders in sizzling, shouting white spouts or spread out shallow over the wide yellow rocks with hardly a sound, or fell *plunk* from a precipice to a pool below that could be

dived into from suicide heights, heart stopping completely
on the way down, smacking the surface of the water, arrow-
ing in, down, down into the temple-freezing pool, finally
starting up again, lungs bursting, finally breaking water feet
first so a corpse would appear to be coming up, my father
standing on the side of the rock waterfall pool and calling,
"You fool, you're going to break your neck," but smiling
pride all the time he said it.

His country was lakes of blue-white fog, lying in the
valleys of an early morning, or the sun setting hot and red
behind a cold blue peak. His country was sudden sheer drop-
offs, and my brother and I made the best of them, running
ahead and finding one coming that looked as if it sheered
right down five thousand feet. Actually hidden from view
would be a large ledge a few feet down for safe landing.
Once my brother and I decided to scare our father with a
ledge fight, so we started fake wrestling on a dangerous-
looking cliff, and as soon as he came round the bend in the
trail and spotted us struggling away in such a precarious
spot, I hauled back and took a wild swing at my brother,
missing his jaw by a quarter inch. He staggered back,
seemed to lose his footing and went right off the precipice
backwards with a terrible scream that kept on even
after he had disappeared from view but then faded
off to a valley of silence. I struck a pose of horror.
My father was approaching, mouthing oaths. Had we
finally pierced his thick hide and struck some terror

into his heart? He seemed impervious, whatever lengths we took to scare him. For this was not the way he saw himself or his sons dying, falling off mountains or plunging into shallow pools from high cliffs. He had been doing things like that all his life, and now so had we, that part of us. Death or mutilation was simply out of the question—we were too strong and too fast and too good with our reflexes to have stupid, fatal accidents.

At home, sometimes, sitting in his big armchair by the fire, my father's eyes could grow gray and sad as he considered his life and worried and was even afraid, but he was never sad or fearful on our trips. Rough, big, clean, virgin country did something for his soul which made him full of courage and laughter, and cares were thrown to the wind. His country tested his mettle and made his body strain to its limits and left him wonderfully exhausted at the end of a day, as he always thought a day should end, with something difficult having been accomplished, something hard and huge surmounted. No, in his country we couldn't frighten a single bone in his body, however devious the plans my brother and I could come up with.

"My poor brother," I yelled. "What have I done?" Maybe this was pouring it on a little thick. It was hard to keep a straight face. So up came my brother's face, peeping over the fake cliff, and our father would growl a little at us and tell us that someday we were going to give him apoplexy. But the trouble with warnings like that was that round the next bend or over the next boulder, he might be pulling the next hokum. We called it "jouing the fou"—just being idiots together—and we were jouing the fou, all three of us, all the time, all over those mountains during those summers. We gave nicknames to other hikers we passed on the trails or met at the huts along the Presidential and Franconia ranges. Black Underwear was a squat little man who actually wore pitch-black undershorts; we saw them when he was changing for a swim. Dirty Underwear was another man. The Boy Who Wasn't Particular was called that because of the horrible-looking girl he had—he showed us a picture of her—and he was going to run all the way down Lafayette for a date with her that night. We met a nice man named Harold who was doing the Presidential Range alone, so we hooked up together, but the three of us just couldn't call our new friend Harold, he looked so much like another man named George we knew, so we called Harold George behind his back for a few days, along with a lot of hysterical giggling, and finally we just came out and told him he looked too much like George not to be George and that's what we were going to call him.

George was a little surprised when he first saw the three of us go through our burp routine. We were all resting beside a stream, ladling up water in our hands and having an ice-cold drink, when my father chimed in with a long, rolling, delicious beauty of a belch that even had an echo to it. "Hundy!" the cry rang out from my brother and me in unison. We'd said it before our father had said "no Hundy," and that meant we could pummel our vile father with muscle punches, really hard ones with the knuckle of the middle finger out if we felt like it, and we didn't have to let up until he had said the names of six kinds of dogs. My father would usually sit there and take it as he thought up dogs with long names like Afghanistan or Welsh Terrier, shrugging off our blows all the time as if we were nothing more than flies batting him with our wings. But when my brother or I was the burper caught red-handed by a lightning-fast "Hundy" and on the receiving end of some machine-gun arm work, we had the six dogs down to a science. Peke, Dane, Pug, Chow, Bull, Toy! A mere six syllables and even they could be shortened to a slurring "piggly-boy."

If a punch happened to be thrown and landed after the last dog had been screamed out, then retaliation was in order, and the one just brutalized could now mete out his own punishment by merely calling "squirrel!" Then he was allowed to throw his mulligans until he had heard the names of five kinds of nuts. "Peapecanwalhorsechestnut" could be mouthed in under a second. Of course my father would go in for slow almonds and roasted cashews. All this nonsense was named after Hundred, our old pointer, who wasn't much at sniffing out birds but was pretty good at burping and other noises himself, and smells, too, and after Hundy's favorite sport, chasing squirrels.

George caught on pretty soon and didn't mind a sudden

Hundy outbreak, but usually only the three of us knew about it, my father and my brother and me, and that was OK alone or in the mountains or off fishing, but maybe a little peculiar on a train to the city or on the sidewalks of our town—to suddenly have a father whacking away at his son's arm or vice versa with a lot of laughing and crying out in mock pain and strange language thrown in.

I had finished looking at the color slides in the hospital, but I kept some boxes aside, out of the suitcase, to go through again when I was home. These were the fishing pictures. In the early 1940's, out of her earnings from her children's books, my mother had given my father the best birthday present he ever got, better even than the bees she had given him which brought him honey and delight for decades, and that was a membership in a fishing club which owned the headwaters of the famous trout river in the Catskills—the Beaverkill. From then on, he spent most of his summer vacations there and many of his weekends. Friday evenings after work, along with my mother, or one or two of us, or some close friends, he would take the three-hour drive from our hill up into the Catskills, and after a black, bumpy last hour over a steep, rutted dirt road, he would arrive at the farmhouse that acted as the lodge for the club members. He would be up at dawn, taking pictures of the mist rising off the lake below the house, trying to catch in the background the speck of a moose having a morning drink at the far end of the lake. He would be laying out his gear, greasing his line, testing his leaders, picking his favorite flies for the day. He always took his little camera with him to the river to record any particularly lovely sites he might run into, a stretch of water he liked, a certain pool, lunch in the meadow, to make a picture of the catch at the end of the day, the fish, stiff now from lying in his creel, taken from their wrapping of wet ferns and placed in a row in the grass or on a rock.

On one of my early-rising, prowling mornings this December, I got the urge to see the Beaverkill again—I had gone through the pictures too fast in the hospital—so I set my projector up on our kitchen table, propped it up with a lump of sugar so it would shine on a clear spot on the kitchen wall, and then, huddled against the four A.M. cold of the house, I poked on the projector light and slowly began re-living that part of his country, the fishing years.

And it was his country, too, that trout stream, the way the water looked running thinly over yellow pebbles, how a rock ledge fell to the water's edge and made a secret hiding place beneath it for a fish, how the midday sun turned the dry rocks on the banks of the stream white and the trees a bright white-green, and how noon seemed to still the waters and kept the trout from rising. How deep blue was the droplet of a lake that fed the stream, how ruffled just before a storm, how black and still at dusk with a sudden plop of a rise to break the smooth mirror with widening circles into the blackness, and how sunlight looked stretching through the arch of heavy trees, the water lit by occasional smoky spot-lights, turning the brown to glassy yellow, turning the dark ferns on the bank a bright feathery green, turning slabs of bank-rock to aluminum, making a trunk gold, changing a fast open stretch to quicksilver.

He took us there to the headwaters of the Beaverkill and taught us how to cast and how to strike a trout and how to play him and land him without a net and how to kill him clean and fast if he was definitely a keeper—something special—and how to unhook him and let him go if he wasn't.

We would fish apart on different beats of the stream, and my father would always bid my brother and me farewell by wishing us "tight line." Sometimes I would fish a beat without any luck at all and my mind would wander away from fish and nets and flies, and I would find myself whipping the water with my line, scaring any nice rainbow or brown that might be waiting below surface, and soon out of carelessness my line would get tangled in a tree. Fed up and tired, I would fold up early and come sneaking upstream on my father, so he had no idea I was in the neighborhood, and I would sit on a bank downstream from him and just watch as he worked the water, deadly serious, stopping now to change a fly, now to dip a soggy one in his little glass bottle of home-mixed paraffin and gasoline to make it float. I would watch him spy a deep pool underneath an overhanging stump, see him slowly wading up upon it to get it in range, see him wipe a thumb over his tongue in anticipation, the water coursing past his bare legs and soaking the leg bottoms of his khaki shorts, his sneakered feet searching for firm footing.

How could a man, I wondered, be so absorbed with a stretch of stream and a little invisible fish that probably wasn't even there? Why would he put up with the cold of the water for so long and the slimy, stony bottom that stubbed toes and stumbled legs? How could he evacuate from his mind all other thoughts for hours on end, focusing only on the possibilities of what his line and fly and skill and cunning could lure from the shining waters? It was his medicine, I guess, just as the mountains had been. It was his cure for the disease of the marketplace in which he worked, his magic herb to heal the wounds from all that smoky city worry, all that pavement-elevator-office-telephone tedium. But it was more than medicine. It was his religion. God did not dwell in cities. He inhabited the wilds, and it was His water rushing by, His fish hiding under the bubbly spill or hugging the side of a sluiceway, and it was His man with rod and fly in the late afternoon sun. The stalk was a rite. Anything less than deadly concentration would have been an act of heresy.

I watched now as the line began to sizzle in the air in great looping sweeps, and when he had enough line out to reach the pool, he suddenly flicked his wrist again and the fly settled over the dark hole without a ripple. He never even noticed the horde of gnats around his head or the late-afternoon sun working over his bare back. He never took his eyes from the pool, from the fly floating gently back toward him now, and he frowned, so intense was his expectation of something big to come, not just any old fish, but a big and smart one who would not be fooled by just any old fly alighting on the evening dinnertable-water, a great one that might hide all day in the shadows, waiting in the cold deep for the perfect meal, the perfect fly, the perfect wings and landing and skitter over the water of the pool before making the charge for it and even then a fish so smart, so old and wise, that it would give the fly a whack with its tail first to see if it was real, and then my father would whip the rod back again, as if the fly had actually felt the whack of the tail and taken off—and his wrist would work the rod a few times, the wood of the rod gold in the late evening sun, the line a string of yellow sizzling off it back and forth across the water, the leader coming off the line invisible except when sun glinted it silver, the fly searching, stretching, stopping in midflight as the cast was finally made, the fly descending now in a perfect, parachute-like sail down for a quiet landing just where the tail had plopped a moment before, sitting there proudly, that royal coachman of the evening. Then suddenly the strike. A tight line, a bent rod, a darting shadow across the dappled stream, as the reel whirred out line and my father trembled at the wonder of it all.

.   .   .

Dawn arrived as I watched those images of my life, his life, against my kitchen wall, and with it, those images became lighter, less defined, the colors faded. In the last few moments before the sun rose and began streaming its winter beams through the kitchen window and onto the wall, obliterating my past completely, I flashed out a few pictures from way far back, ten years before the Beaverkill, the summer months in Maine. The house was warm now. I threw off the coat I had wrapped myself in and two or three times I got up to touch a spot on the wall where a sailboat was flying before the wind, or to pick out a person with my finger, someone I had forgotten had ever lived. I even talked aloud, calling out a name when I felt like it. Was this a last, desperate look at life? Was it holding on? Was it wanting to feel, to touch, to have, to be? Yesterday's images grew even dimmer on the wall as the sun glinted through the window. Still I could make them out, the Maine vacations. Yes, his country was coastline, too. Was ocean. Was island off the coast of Maine where my father took us for his two weeks of vacation, we staying on for five or six weeks with my mother, he commuting there on weekends. That wasn't easy. Monday through Thursday night he lived alone on the hill, working all week in the steaming city of New York, working at his job in the woolen industry, and then on Friday evenings he would throw the cloth aside and get into his car and start out for Maine. There were no superhighways then, no turnpikes, just Route 1, and he churned along with the trucks for fourteen straight hours, all night long, aiming for Maine. What could he have thought of during those hours? As all that dark road got eaten up, time after time, his headlights piercing through Connecticut, up through Massachusetts, slicing through a corner of New Hampshire, on into Maine itself, twisting along the coastline, through the little towns that bordered the sea, watching the sun rise over Brunswick or Bath or Boothbay Harbor or Penobscot Bay? Did he think of us, nestled in our island beds, waiting for his Saturday morning arrival? Was he ever frightened by the distance or the dark? Did he once think of death? Or did he just enjoy the coming, the feat of the journey, the extent of the physical exertion?

He arrived in the nick of time to catch the Saturday morning ferry to the island, and we would meet him at the dock at eight, his smile looking as if he'd slept the whole night, although he'd only snatched a catnap on the boat.

The weekend would be freezing swims and howling sails and suck holes deep in the rocks spraying their whale-spout surf into the sky, and fierce caps of white water on a windy sea, and seaweed, and barnacles and blueberries and pine and the blue rage of a high wind and the fierce, sad streak of the Sunday evening sun coming at us out of the west over the quieting waters as the ferry left and we watched his wave until it was a speck, giving it back with all our might, as he was off for another all-night drive to be back in the city in time for Monday work.

❖❖❖❖❖❖❖❖❖❖❖❖❖❖❖❖❖❖❖❖❖❖❖❖❖❖❖❖❖❖❖❖❖❖❖❖

His Special Way of Life

THE CONTENTS OF MY FATHER'S DESK BECAME A source of many little insights, over the winter months of my convalescence, insights into the nature of this man who had helped make me, bring me up, teach me, who struggled in my behalf, sacrificed, cared for me, finally set me off on my own course with enthusiasm and encouragement and the dreams of the mighty things a person could do and make and become in this world.

Among the desk's contents was a stack of twenty-five tiny leatherbound diary-notebooks. Each Christmas, my father would get a new one for the upcoming year—black, with almost tissue-thin pages, the whole booklet not much bigger than a pack of matches. And before the first of January he would transfer onto the dated entry pages—each little page given over to three days—all the birthdays and anniversaries he wanted to keep remembering for still another year, the special dates he wanted to know about in advance and do something about when the time came, his own engagement date, always marked with the number of years that had passed since that proposal and acceptance had been made; the birthdays, and later the death days, too, of his mother and his father: "Dad" and beside that word an x on every June 14 after 1934, and another x and "Mother" on November 3 after 1941. He would also transfer into the new little book all the current sizes of dresses and shirts and shoes and hats and pants and gloves of each member of his family, to be referred to for Christmas and birthday presents, and in the very back of the new book, he would copy all the names and addresses and telephone numbers of the people who were most important to him.

On New Year's Day he would write the last entry of the year just finished, and that would usually be a New Year's Eve skating party at the Low's pond, and he would put the old booklet into one of the drawers of the desk and bring out the new diary and make a first entry in it. There was only room enough for a few words each day, but he never missed filling in one of those dated, half-inch-high spaces from the late 1930's, when he started keeping these miniature records, until the last full year of his life—1962—when the entries started to become spotty in June and disappeared altogether in November.

He got two weeks off from his job each July or August, and the entries for those periods told the brief histories of our climbing and fishing and island and seashore vacations. "Climbed Giant Mountain, climbed Haystack"; "Tuckerman to *Lake of the Clouds*"; "19 mile brook trail to Carter";

"Packed into Zeeland. Swam in falls all afternoon"; "Saw bear track"; "Franconia Range—Lafayette, Lincoln, Haystack, Liberty, Flume to Indian Head"; "Home." Or "Flat Rock Pool—one 12 inch brown"; "below stone dam, one rainbow"; "rain all day, seven keepers all put back."

Except for those fleeting summer vacations, the entries in those little books were mostly about our hill, about chores my father had accomplished that day, or that morning, or that evening, on paths, on trees, on the house, in his flower garden.

In the desk, too, at the bottom of a drawer, untouched for decades, had been the drawings my father had made of the garden he wanted. We had moved to our house on the hill when I was four. In front of the house, below the view of the valley, was a jungle of trees and bushes and wilderness. My father had looked at it from our front steps and in some way knew what could be fashioned there. It would take thought and planning and patience and infinite strength and dedication. But there was no question in his mind that he could do it. As he looked, he was remembering his mother's great formal gardens at the mansion where he had grown up in Massachusetts. In the desk there was a photograph of those gardens, with their clipped grass paths and carefully edged borders, their scallop-shaped beds, their hedges, their marble benches to be sat upon for meditative viewing. The setting of our hill was altogether different, a sloping wild tangle of growth to deal with rather than those flat, sweeping, carefully-honed stretches. Still the flower bed designs he drew were, in shape, if not in size, exact replicas of the Massachusetts ones. Although he did not have the money or the help or the stately house or the right kind of land, he was determined to recreate as closely as he could that graceful setting in which beautiful things grew in his boyhood.

His drawings called for two rectangular rose beds separated by a white marble bench at the lower end of the garden. Yes, the very same marble bench that had occupied one of the sitting nooks in his mother's garden. Also inherited was a green Ali Baba-sized Italian jar that he placed at the top of his garden beneath a giant border locust tree.

Stretching at right angles up the hill from those first two rose beds, the plans showed two beds of mixed flowers, each the shape of a long curved bean, but running in opposite ways so that one had its fat end down, the other up. Now the drawings showed two more rose beds, half-moon scallops, and after them, stretching to the top of the garden toward our house, two more of the bean-shaped mixed beds. For the rose gardens, there were detailed plans which indicated that each bush had been chosen in advance and placed carefully, by name, so that a calculated pattern of colors would be created and each bed would have its own character, its own central prize bushes and its complementing ones.

That first winter he laid his plans, waiting for thaw. Then he struck—first with ax, slaughtering the trees out of the space in front of our house—ninety feet down, thirty across. He carved it from the forest, that garden space, and when the trees were finally down and the stumps hauled out by the brute of his back and the hard land loosened by pickax and the soil tilled and sifted through an old screen door to get rid of every rock and impurity, then he decided his earth had to be enriched before planting. Half a mile away, almost at the bottom of the hill, was a sheep barn, long unused. He would load the three of us in the wheelbarrow—his Nannie-Kins, his Doodlebug, his Peel (that was me) —and ride us down there, all of us jumbled up and wailing and laughing at the hard shocks when the iron wheel clanked over a stone or hit a rut; and when we got to the barn door, he would suddenly dump us out like mice.

Inside on the cement floor of the sheep pens was a hard, thick, dry crust of manure. He would take his half-moon cutter and slice out wedges of the stuff and then he would scoop them up with a flat coal shovel and fill the wheelbarrow to overflowing. All the time we would be diving from a rafter into the hay in the loft, we would be tightrope walking on a thin steel bar that stretched high above the hay to help support the barn roof, we would be doing trapeze acts, climbing the silo walls, lowering ourselves through a trap door to the empty horse stalls in the barn's lower level, having dung fights in the abandoned chicken coops. We would be sneaking out over a beam to drop like commandos onto my father below, to try to wrestle him to the floor. He would shake us off, put a last slab of manure on his load, lift up the handles and begin the long trip back, up the steep hill behind the barn, on up past the apple trees, the pear trees, the cherry trees that bordered the road, past the pastures, past the old ice house at the foot of one of the fields, into a tunnel of tall trees that led to our house and his new garden. He made the trip a hundred times that first spring and summer, mixing that rich fertilizer with his sifted earth in those five-foot-deep beds, stone lined at the bottoms for proper drainage, chomping the manure deep down into the soil that was going to work for him so many years.

When the time was just right, he planted, roses at first, ordered with care from a catalog, each with its own regal name—a Duchess of Wellington, a Mrs. P. S. Dupont, Talisman, Pinocchio, McGrady's Yellow, Mme. Butterfly, Herbert Hoover, Lady Alice Stanley, Mrs. Aaron Ward, Golden Rapture. He wrote the name of each rose on a little white wood marker and wired it to the trunk of the bush.

The other beds were not planted with so much care. They always seemed a wild tangle of flowers, a jungle, with only the order of size to them—hollyhocks and sunflowers craning their necks in the back, way down to pansies and violets bordering the front. In between there were lilies of all variety—regal lilies, tiger lilies, lilies of the valley dripping their white bells amid their rich-green vegetable leaves; there were marigolds and crocus, zinnias and chrysanthemums, phlox and petunias and some special "true" Solomon's seal brought from his mother's garden in Massachusetts. In the heat of midsummer the garden exploded into slashes of color and shapes—the splendor of a yellow iris with its thin brown dangling ears, the yellow pistol rods shooting out of the bright white upturned nun's-cap blossoms of the regal lilies, the blue confusion of violets run wild.

When the beds were done and planted, he dug up arborvitae trees and planted them to make a hedge at the back of the garden, and he made fence posts out of the trunks of small locust trees and fence rails out of saplings, and planted climbing roses all along that new fence so that soon his garden was hemmed in from all the wildness on either side. And he forced a lawn to grow down the middle between the beds. And for the rest of his life in the morning before leaving for the city and in the evening upon his return and over the weekends, whenever the season was right, he worked in his garden, spraying and planting, cultivating and picking, watering and loving all the beautiful things that he had helped make.

That was why he waged war with winter, he loved his garden so. He always fought winter mightily, digging his way out of the deep snow, lashing chains onto the rear tires of his old cars, first Celeste, then Chowdog, cursing the ice storms that sheathed the branches of his beloved trees with unbearable, gleaming weight. When the temperature struck low, the streak of mercury outside the dining room window hardly shoving up at all from its little silver sleeping-pool, then the ice would not go away for weeks and he would

put hay and licks of salt out for the deer and sunflower seeds
for the birds and he would worry about all the wild animals
on our hill until the melt began. He hated hunters. They
seemed to have the same mindless, cruel intent as winter
itself. Whenever he heard the smack of a rifle in the distant
woods, he would explode all over the hill, and if he didn't
find the offender and shake him off the land with a clenched
fist, he would certainly leave no game behind, my father's
swath through the trees was such a loud and fierce one.

One winter meant preparing for the next, and so the air
was filled with the clean sound of ax blade sinking into hard
wood, the chime of sledgehammer against wedge, the slow,
sinewy crackle of wood fiber as a piece opened up. In the
winter my father was a man of leather and canvas and laced
boots. He did not seem to need wool or fur or parkas or
scarves or earmuffs or lined gloves, or any of the other things
normal people use to deal with the cold. On a stinging day
he would lace up skates for a whole shivering bunch of us
and then his own without a single finger turning numb. He
could pack dry snowballs with bare hands or roll huge wet
ones for a fort or grip the metal of a Flexible Flyer on a
downhill race and never seem to feel the cold. Snow could
pile on his hair or get packed between his neck and canvas
collar or ease down his boots, and it only was relief to him,
for he laid it up to hot blood, and at meals he cooled that
blood down with two quarts of ice water he drank from a
green glass flower vase. Even when ice formed on his ears

and eyebrows, it just seemed to keep that heat in. Steam bellowed from his mouth and in sudden snorts from his nostrils. You could never tell when he got back in the cellar after winter work and shook off all the snow and hung up the canvas jacket on a nail beside the furnace whether it was wet through from blizzard or from sweat.

Of course, the laconic little entries in his notebooks never recorded any of this. They were merely his tidy way of keeping the record, his record. Sometimes there were luncheon appointments, or reminders for meetings—business meetings in the city or meetings at the school he and my mother had started out in the country, or Community Chest meetings which he ran, or library meetings which he headed, or vestry meetings at our church, or Harvard Club meetings which he presided over, or meetings at the hospital of which he was president.

There was never any emotion in the words he used. On August 6, 1945, a Monday, "The Atomic Bomb" with no comment. The next day, "Dith fell out the window." Dith was our new baby—Edith, named after my mother's mother. She was eight when she had fallen out of the second-story window beside her bed in the middle of the night and she would have been killed if a bayberry bush had not somehow broken her sleeping head-first fall. My father patted that bush many times after that, and thanked it, and thanked God for it, for he could not have lost that baby of his, she was the apple of his eye—no, his "peach," he liked that word better to describe somebody who was favorite to him, or another word he used for people he thought quite a bit of, she was his "corker."

The little diary notebooks did not tell things like how my father hated clothes, how he yearned for summer so he could go around again in a pair of khaki shorts held up by a heavy leather belt, a red handkerchief for sweat stuck under the belt at one hip—that was all. They did not say how scared he was when he first got his bees and how he dressed up in hip boots and a cloak of mosquito netting his first time inspecting the brood, and how glad he was when he got his first sting and didn't die from it—he'd read in the paper about someone who died from a bee sting. And the notebooks didn't tell how much he loved the fig tree that his barber had given him, how he had to wrap the entire tree in burlap every winter and then bend it over and bury it so it wouldn't freeze and die, and how Edith was the only girl at her boarding school who got fresh figs straight from a tree when her parents came to visit.

Reading those little books now, it is impossible to tell one year from the next through the entries. Each winter had its "big snow" and a few "the worst storm in history." The winter entries tended to be terse, gloomy. Each spring the comments seemed to lighten, there were more adjectives to show the joy that he shared with the earth coming alive again. Summer was heaven to him and fall a saddening. Decades slipped together. Taken as a whole, the entries told

of his own special way of life. They told of simple things—
weather, work, accomplishments, beauty. . . .

"Mist, overcast"; "beautiful cool day"; "cut and burned";
"chopped out pool path"; "worked on stump"; "sawed";
"fig tree unburied, nice rainbow after storm"; "cleaned shop,
spread manure"; "attacked back of house"; "scythed bee
place"; "dug left bed"; "burned"; "the last of the stump,
filled in hole"; "tied climbers"; "mist and cold" "first mow-
ing of lawn"; "trimmed edges of gardens"; "switched hive
bodies"; "first cleaning of pool"; "heavenly spring day";
"seeded first annual bed"; "sprayed roses"; "terribly hot—
98 degrees"; "seeded stump place"; "showed color slides";
"raked and mowed"; "thunderstorm"; "porch furniture
away"; "buried fig tree"; "Harvard-Yale game"; "first
snow"; "chains on both cars"; "hilled roses"; "skated at
Low's Pond"; "sawed and chopped"; "burned"; "mist."

All My Family

HOME FROM THE HOSPITAL AND THINKING OF Christmas, I decided to make photograph albums for my mother and my brother and my two sisters. They would be made up of prints from the best of my father's color slides plus a selection from the hundreds of other snapshots of our childhood my mother had taken. What a sight—me cross-legged on the floor of my study, practically drowning in a sea of pictures. My wife would open the door, look for a moment, shake her head and retreat. I was lost in the past. So many faces and postures and poses and antics and just plain scenes of a growing-up family, records that had come from so many pressed index fingers which had snapped camera shutters and let fleeting moments of light through a lens.

Who was that little runt with the proud angelic smile, brown mussed hair, a worm in his hand to stick down my back, striped shirt, stocking cap, thumbs hooked under belt? Ken, who when he first saw a Good Humor man said, "Gee, Mum, Dad would be perfect for *that*." Could the gentle person who had visited me in the hospital and brought me all our father's slides, could he have ever been that little twerpy toad of a muscled brother staring out at me from the pictures?

And what about those two girls who showed up so much in the photographs? Nancy, forty-two now, living outside of Boston with her husband and their six children. "Please," she wrote me, "just because you're home from the hospital, don't take chances. You'll be so happy to be home, you might just sneak out in the kitchen, if Katharine's out, or just saunter outside to rake a bit or some other idiocy, or just 'easily' take the stairs to see Sandra in her room, when you know you shouldn't do such things for ages." Was this written by the same little girl I used to know, who went through pigtails, hair ribbons, teeth bands, face lotions, knee socks, kerchiefs, two-piece bathing suits, roses in her hair, who had numberless tantrums and bewitched as many boys while we grew up side by side on the hill?

And the other girl, the baby of the family, with a husband and two children now. I got a letter from her, too, with another dose of advice. Who did that little imp think she was, who not so long ago was my slave? I had taught her so carefully. "Who knows best, Edith?" . . . "Phil knows best." . . . "Who is the greatest in the world, Edith?" . . . "Phil is the greatest." That smiling, cunning baby girl with Band-aids always on her knees, whom my brother and I taught football and fighting, who was our prize, who was absolutely doted on by my father, who was left on the hill when the rest of us went off to school and college and marriage, left to do most of her growing up without brothers and sisters around. "It may be simple-minded to remind you," Edith wrote, "but 1) you're alive; 2) you're young; 3) you've got a sense of humor and an island in Maine; 4) this enforced rest will be a wonderful time to *THINK*."

And could the twinkling young mother, brandishing a stirring spoon, striking a hokum pose for the flash-bulbed camera before basting a turkey, could she possibly be the same short-winded, adoring, fiercely willed, lonely, loyal, overly generous, always worried, always working, nimble-minded, talented graying mother who took the train out from the city to see me at the hospital, stuffed my room with presents, kept in touch each day by phone, cared so desperately?

And my father. Was my true picture of him formed in his last year of life when he faced his crippling, fatal illness with such massive dignity and courage, his face rounded and puffed from the excess of liquid in his body, his eyes pinched and tired with pain. Or did the real picture go back to these early photographs—to the young man with the fine-grained white skin, the nut-brown eyes, the lean, strong, six-foot, 195-pound body, topped by that quick smile? Or was it somewhere in between, during the middle of his life, when he was crushed with business worries, on the brink of defeat?

Where did the truth lie? Now? Yesterday? In the distant
past? I did not know. But as I dived into the flood of old
family photographs, I chose again to see if memory, with
all its sharp pictures, all its dulled and muddied parts, all its
romance and colorings, could somehow shed some rays of
light upon the questions that my head and heart were asking.

My older sister and I could be best friends or worst
enemies, whichever mood struck us at the moment. There
was a loose board underneath the door that separated our
rooms which we could pull out, and that made a whisper
well for using after we were supposed to be in bed. Nancy
was a year older, so I didn't pester her too much except one
year when we found out she was terrified of death; then my
brother and I decided to dig her grave. We got shovels
and a pickax out of my father's workshop and we cleared
the vines and weeds off a patch of ground in back of the
house, a place she could easily see from the bathroom window, and we took her measurements with a tape, explaining
to her we needed to be exact so there wouldn't be any un-
necessary digging, and we started in, picking and shoveling
—a hole five feet long and two across. She thought it was a
joke at first, but when she saw we weren't fooling, we were
going to keep on digging there until her grave was ready,
that began to upset her a bit and she started talking about it
to our mother. "Mum," she would say, "you know what
those dreadful boys are doing? Do you know what they're

actually doing? They are digging a grave. For me, they say. *My* grave. Isn't that the most disgusting thing you've ever heard? Would you please do something about it? Would you kindly talk to them. It's not very nice, what they're doing."

We just dug away until the grave was ready, the deep sides flat and the bottom square like a professional grave, with a good peaked pile of earth beside it to shovel on quickly when we had her in there. And then for the next few days we'd drop hints as to exactly the time and place the abduction was going to take place, how the hands would be tied behind the back and the ankles bound with wire and the mouth gagged with adhesive tape. It would probably be in the dark when our parents went out to dinner some night and no one on the hill would be around to hear any screaming. And we'd be sure not to knock her on the head, knock her out or stun her or anything, because knowing you were being buried alive was the best part of it, having the dirt piled up on top of you, shovelful after shovelful, feeling it fall on your face and covering up your nose, we told her, and trying to breathe and not being able to with all that dark dirt weight over your chest and lips and face and everywhere.

"Disgusting brothers!" she would say as she passed us in the hall. "I hate you."

"Just wait," we told her. "The right time will come. The grave is open now and fresh and ready and waiting."

And that's the way it stayed for a couple of months until my father filled the grave in on the pretense someone would trip in there and break his leg, but actually I think he was just taking sides with my sister, he was always on her side, he seemed to like her quite a bit, calling her his Tweets, his Nannie-Kins, driving her to school miles out of his way to the station when she could have taken the bus, presenting her with the first garden sweetheart rose of the spring, sweeping her off her feet when he got home at night and twirling her around so her skirts flew in a dancing hug.

There were times when I thought she was worth it; she had a nice streak to her, like keeping Anna's breath for about ten years. Anna was a nurse who took care of us once for a month, and we got to like her, so my sister made Anna breathe into a bottle before she left and Nancy kept that bottle on a shelf in her room for years after, remembering Anna by it. Of course, any time my brother and I wanted to get her mad, all we'd have to do is say we'd taken out the stopper, not only taken it out but blown into the bottle ourselves—so she didn't have Anna's breath at all in there, she had her darling, adorable brothers' halitosis on her shelf.

My brother was two years younger than I, so I didn't have to be so kind to him. Ken was a little spunk of a guy who wore stupid shirts, and his pants were always hanging off him. I had a little thing I did with him whenever I was feeling a bit lordly. I would tell him I could mix a magic potion that would turn anyone into the strongest person in the world. He said he didn't believe it. I said just wait and went into the bathroom and locked the door and mixed up a glass of very soapy water with some mint-flavored cod liver oil in it, a bit of Vince toothpowder, and anything else that was around the shelves. I opened the door and showed it to him and then I told him I was going to drink it, put it right up to my lips and made shows of drinking, then dodged back into the bathroom and let the stuff fly into the bathtub, back out again with the empty glass to my lips as if I was just draining off the last mouthful. "It tastes awful," I told him, "but it really works." Then I would show him how my muscles were getting bigger and stronger and I was getting as powerful as a gorilla. In fact, now I grabbed him and threw him on the floor and told him I was sorry, I had to restrain myself after drinking Zo-Zo or I might kill someone. I better run around until it worked off. After a couple of circles of the house I was back up there in his bedroom saying, "Well, that's better, it's almost worked off now; boy, you feel so strong after that Zo-Zo you could tear down a tree or anything." My brother would look at me with envy. And when the time was just ripe, the look just envying enough, I would say, "By the way, would you like to try a little Zo-Zo?" He would be dying to, of course, and so I would go lock myself in the bathroom again and mix up a really strong batch and bring it out. He would take a sip and make a face.

"It doesn't taste good, but just drink it," I would tell him.

"It works wonders." He would force down half the glass and gag. "Do you feel the strength coming?" I would ask him. "Here, try to knock me down."

My brother would put down the glass and flex his muscles and give me a push and I would go sailing across the room, crash into the closet and totally collapse.

"Hey, what are you trying to do, kill somebody?" I would shout at him. "That Zo-Zo's more powerful than I thought."

I would get up and limp back over and he would grab my arm and I would make it all limp so he could easily get a half nelson, and pretty soon he had me down and crying for mercy.

"Don't drink another drop of that stuff," I would say. "You'll murder someone." And he'd quickly let go and hop up and drain off the rest of the Zo-Zo. I don't know how he forced it down, without throwing up—and the Zo-Zo business went on for maybe a year before he caught on.

Even without Zo-Zo he was a strong little brother and we fought a lot, but whenever we had a real fight, I mean all-out, to the finish, no holds barred, that meant anything goes— from kicking, choking, scratching, hair-pulling, slugging of any kind—whenever we had that kind of a fight, we had a pact that there would be no crying. We even called them "no-crying fights." I made him sign a pact for no-crying fights because if there was a lot of crying on his part after one, then my mother would get furious at me, say I was picking on my little brother, and send me to my room.

Once, I remember, she found us in the middle of a no-crying fight really going at it, tearing away at each other like mad dogs, and she screamed us apart and told us that as soon as our father got home we would receive a terrible spanking. She sent us to our room to await his arrival and the punishment.

Now my father wasn't any good at spanking at all, my brother and I knew that. But our mother's voice this time had a quality of meaning business in it, so we decided we had to do something to change the subject when he got home. We thought for a while and then we got the bright idea of making dummies in our beds. We got pillows for bodies and rolled up towels for legs and bunched up sweaters for heads and put this all in the shape of two bodies underneath our blankets. And we tied string around the pillows and got underneath the beds. We could hear my father coming in the front door, and my mother telling him about us in a sharp voice. We could tell he was hesitating, but I guess she finally had him convinced, because he came right up the stairs and went to his bathroom for a hairbrush and in a moment he appeared at the door of our room. We started pulling at the strings, making the bodies look as if they were breathing.

"You two boys are going to get a spanking," my father said. "Get up out of bed and come over here."

Not a noise from us, just some pulls of the string, more breathing looks.

"You can hear me perfectly well," my father said. "Get up and come here. Your mother says you have been behaving dreadfully."

Now he was beside the bed and whopping off the blankets. Dummies! We couldn't help giggling from underneath. We crawled out. My father was trying to keep a straight face. "First you," he said, catching me by the arm and trying to put me across his knee. He raised the hairbrush and brought it down and it made a clomping whack as it hit the Oz book I had shoved beneath the seat of my pants for final precaution. He just couldn't keep a straight face. I think he tried for a minute to get the book out but I was wriggling like a trout and finally all three of us were getting the giggles—and that was the end of the only spanking I can remember, except we did get a lecture about the fighting, and my mother was told the matter had been taken care of.

Nancy and Ken and I treated our new sister Edith differently from the way we treated each other. For years we had been wishing for a baby, wishing for one every time we passed a haywagon or pulled a turkey bone or blew out our birthday candles. But Ken always claimed that he had got Edith for us by wishing on a graveyard. We passed one in the car and he held his breath until he was red in the face and he wished hard. Two weeks later when our mother announced that she was going to have a baby, Ken revealed that he and the graveyard had been responsible.

Everybody said Edith looked just like Dad. They said

they had never seen such a resemblance. But my father insisted he couldn't see the slightest likeness. That was strange because he was always going out of his way to find things she had that were his. He would spread out his big fingers next to her little ones. "Poor child," he would say, "she has her father's square hand and chunky fingers." But he smiled foolishly as if he thought she wouldn't do so badly with his hand.

My father spent every second he could with Edith. In the morning when he was dressing for work he would go over to where she was lying and gurgling and he would always give her his rolled-up socks that he had just got from the bureau drawer. He would let her hold them a minute, even though she hadn't learned to hold onto anything yet, so pretty soon they would roll away, but my father said he enjoyed his day better if Edith just held his socks for him even for a second in the morning.

When he was dressed, he carried her down to the table and ate his breakfast with her sitting on his lap. At the end of breakfast he stuck his finger in the honey and put it in Edith's mouth, and then he would say very loud, looking quite delighted and proud, "Whew! Stop! She's biting me. She's just like a beaver."

Every morning after breakfast, like clockwork, Dad danced with Edith. He carried her into the living room and lifted her high over his head. Then while we all stood in a circle and sang a waltzing tune, he whirled her around up near the ceiling. After he was finished he brought her down and whispered in her ear, "Thank you, that was a lovely dance." After the dance one morning Nancy said, "Edith is going to have an awful disappointment when she finds out that her beaus are only going to walk her around on the floor instead of fly her in the air."

Sometimes in the mornings, when the sun came shining through the glass prisms of the candlesticks on our mantel making rainbows on the rug, Edith and Dad would lie side by side and dabble their fingers in the colors. On those mornings my father took the 8:06 instead of the 7:55 train. Usually he could get their dance in and make the 7:55 but on rainbow-catching mornings he needed nine extra minutes.

In those early hill days it was my brother who summed up our feelings about Edith best. "I'd like to keep her exactly how she is this minute," Ken said. "I'd like to shellac her."

My mother despised the outside just as much as my father loved it. She liked being boxed in by house or city. Fresh country air just didn't agree with her, she always claimed. She told us if she had her wish she would live in one of those little cubbyholes in Grand Central Station where you can lock your bag for twenty-five cents. She said she'd just climb in there and close the door and be extremely happy with those close walls and no weather at all to worry about. My mother and father found out how different they were in this respect on their honeymoon when he chose to take her to a small woodsy camp near Monticello in Virginia where she watched him lie and splash like a huge white tadpole in an outsize brook, where they had bad food and rode old jogging plugs of horses through the woods. They had spent one night en route in a hotel in Washington, D.C., and my mother had longed to stay there, in an exciting and interesting city, not the horrible woods. But my father had hated the hotel, the city, had longed to get to the real heart of his week's honeymoon, in the woods and fields.

Later on, as their marriage settled into a tacit agreement, each to give in to the other on the little things that did not matter, they let their sense of humor enter into the problems of daily life. She would sit upstairs in the window backed by her thousands of Civil War books calling to my father down in the garden with his roses, "Come in, come in!" And he would smile and call back, "Come out, come out!" with no resulting change in their positions.

Of all the children my mother was closest to Nancy, although you wouldn't have known it. They both cared so much about every little thing, and that made them clash all the time, and a good clash meant going at each other like crazy people. About any subject at all. Little finicky subjects usually. Squabbling and squawking about practically nothing, practically anything. There were times when one just couldn't say or do anything that didn't aggravate the other.

"You are wicked and rude," my mother would tell Nancy.

"And you will not slam doors right straight in people's faces."

"It's *my* door to *my* room and it will be slammed whenever it feels like being slammed in whosever face might be lurking on the other side, trying to destroy my privacy and butting into my affairs and prying into my private life."

"You had better watch what comes out of your mouth, Nancy. You are a member of this family and not a wild animal."

They were very close, though, and my sister confided all her innermost secrets, all her affairs of the heart, to my mother, and my mother in turn told Nancy what she thought and helped guide her.

I kept more to myself; nobody was going to know what was going on inside me, about school, about hurts, about dreams, about loves, about anything. Ken confided in our father. He really should have been the first-born boy and got my father's name because he looked just like him, the same face, the same solid build, the same determinations, and he liked to do the same simple outdoor things my father did, while I liked those things only occasionally, and did not look like him at all. The only thing my father and I had in common, it seemed, was that we had the same favorite color—yellow.

My mother could get angry at my brother and me, too. Especially if her concentration was suddenly broken by some lavish, wiseacre noise of ours. Other transgressions that brought on varying degrees of recrimination might include making rabbit ears or nose-thumbs behind the backs of aunts or other guests; whipping the thermometer from under our tongues to the steaming radiator to force it up to 102° and keep us out of school for the day; burning a cousin at the stake; bringing home boys whom my mother considered sneaks or bad-mouths, and that included practically all my friends; dragging our feet like cripples in the market; spitting; teasing; having blasting gunfights all over the house, using pointed fingers for pistols and clutching stomachs, staggering, doubling over, crumpling onto the floor, gurgling and gasping as we died; using tough radio talk like, "You got me, Butch," or "Let's get out of this dump," or telling our sister things like, "So, my fine-feathered friend, you think just 'cause you're older, you're the boss of us. Well, you're not. So you'd better clamp those lips, put that tongue to bed, to put it more bluntly, shut your big ugly trap!"; me smelling everything, a habit I had because I like smells, smelling books before reading and clothes before putting them on, and always smelling food before eating it, which was considered rude at our table; and a lot of other rude table things too when we children were eating alone, like gargling milk or pretending to stab ourselves in the stomach with our dinner knives, or smacking lips on purpose while eating just to drive our sister crazy, or playing tag around the table, or making groaning foghorn B.O. sounds when Nancy reached her arm for something, or scraping food we hated

off our plates and out the window, or copying everything
Nancy said—

"Don't do that, boys!"

"Don't do that, boys!"

"Oh, you're so rude!"

"Oh, you're so rude!"

"Stop it! Shut up! I'll kill you! I'll tell Mummy!"

"Stop it! Shut up! I'll kill you! I'll tell Mummy!"

Those are just a few of maybe five or six thousand little
tricks we had.

"Let the punishment fit the crime," proclaimed my
mother. "If you want to thumb your nose at Auntie, come
out from behind her back and do it to her face." Or, "Spit!.
Go out and spit behind the house to your heart's content
until you'll never want to spit again." And, if it were too
much yelling and yapping and screeching we were doing,
she might, if she were in the mood, set up the worst din you
ever heard, yelling and yapping and screeching louder even
than we had been doing, so that we just stopped and looked
at her in amazement and with a little fear. And when she
was done with her act, she'd ask us how we'd like that kind
of racket going on all the time, and we'd get the point.

My father kept peace in the house. He would settle arguments, calm people down, quiet rough waters. He could put
an arm around one of us and comfort tears away.

"Good guy," he could tell my brother or me, and cuff us
on the back and make us feel right again.

"Easy, Tweets," he could say to our sister, "easy now. It couldn't be that bad."

And after my father got home from work, if we or something else had upset my mother during the day, he would soothe her down too, do the coping, set a course, give her strength. He seemed to have the patience of Job. But that patience broke down over a couple of subjects. One of them was money. My mother's extravagances drove him to distraction, even though they were practically penny extravagances in those days. But things were tight in the thirties and pennies meant everything. My father paid the big bills, like oil and rent and help and schools, and he gave my mother a small check each month to cover everything else—food, clothes, the drugstore, everything. She kept account to the penny: $3.76 for the butcher; $17.25 to the market; $1.50 for boys' haircuts. But every once in a while she went haywire and bought something we couldn't afford—like a birthday present for my father, a beehive from Sears ($7.98) and two pounds of bees plus a queen ($3.67). Then it would take her weeks to pay it off, or else she would come to my father and say she had to have a little more money that month. He would plead with her, softly at first. He just didn't have any more money. He didn't know how we were going to get through the year. His voice rose.

"You must stop spending money that we just don't have!"

"I will try, dear," my mother answered with repentance, "I really will." But she never could, and the scene was repeated over and over all through the years I was growing up.

When anyone made a long-distance call and talked too long, my father would pace the floor back and forth in front of the offender, growling underneath his breath. He could practically see the dollar bills slipping into the mouthpiece of the phone and cascading down its black wire. Electric light bulbs left burning in the daytime angered him, too, as well as pushing up the thermostat in winter to higher than 68 degrees.

Income tax time was always touchy, as night after night, bent over his desk, my father struggled with all the figures, never thinking an accountant might do it better, following the short-form instructions to the letter, never even imagining there might be a legitimate loophole in the long-form fine print that could save him a few dollars. We learned to keep away from the back living room those first two weeks in March. Tension was high then, and sometimes there were poundings on the desk top that made the lamps shake and the crystal dangles on the mantel candlesticks tinkle.

Another thing that aroused my father was careless drivers on the road, and if one seemed to come too close to him in passing, or cut him off, he would set his teeth and pay that driver back, punish him by passing him back even closer and glowering through the window and then cutting him off worse than he had been cut off himself.

On long car rides, my mother would keep my father happy and amused. She would try to make him promise not to punish any more drivers, and she would tell him odd little stories and observations that only her strange, nonsensical mind, that always seemed to end up making sense, could have thought up. Day and night that mind of hers gobbled up quantities of information on every conceivable subject. She could read a page at a single glance and remember everything on it. He marveled at her, he even put up with orders to stop the car this minute, there's a turtle on the road that has to be moved over to the side by hand or somebody's cruel old tire is going to squash him flat, and she'd be out of the car, lifting the turtle to the bank in the direction he was heading and talking to the turtle and telling him not to be naughty again by going out on any more highways. My father even put up with my mother's sense of direction, which was nonexistent, and whenever he let her have the wheel to spell him, which was not very often, he'd give her five minutes before she was dead lost. He had a compass built into him somewhere and knew exactly where he was and which direction he was pointed in, whether night or day, or fog, or completely unknown territory. Sometimes, at home, to test him, we'd blindfold him and spin him around maybe a hundred times and then tell him to point north, and he'd wait a second for the dizziness to wear off and then he'd point due north, not a degree off.

Fortunately for us, my mother didn't have to rely on her sense of direction to get to New York—she just took the

train. And once a year she took each one of us there for a
spree. My mother was the best spree person in the world. She
worked terribly hard at everything she did, but I don't think
she did anything better than giving sprees. Just as in the
children's books she wrote, she seemed to know exactly
what each of us liked and how we liked it, exactly how our
minds worked and what got each one of us excited or left
us bored. A spree day was a magical journey into that mys-
terious city where my father disappeared five days a week.
It was his city, to me, in those days, although I never visited
his office and knew that he disliked being interrupted there
by a phone call from my mother.

My sprees began with my mother driving me to the station
in Morristown, where, waiting for the train, she would have
a talk with her friend, the paper lady. When the train thundered in, I got aboard, and perched by the window, I
watched all the towns as we roared past them, all the familiar
stops, the people moving about, driving in their cars along
roads beside the tracks, looking out of the windows of their
houses and hearing the noise my train made—old people,
young people, boys on bicycles, girls with pigtails, truck
drivers, businessmen, thousands of people whom, I remember thinking, I would see this fleeting time and never see
again, but each one of them would have just as full and important a life as me. And the beat of the train made me dizzy,
sleepy, almost hypnotized me, made me wander back one
generation, then the next, then the next, until I had gotten

way far back, almost to the very beginning, and where had it all begun and how and why? Suddenly, in a grasp, in a glimmer, I seemed to know it all, but it always slipped away, and when a lurch of the train or the conductor calling out a stop woke me, I could never remember the answer. When we got up into the city, the whirlwind of spree things began, racing from one to another, jamming three times as much into that day as any normal people would. We would go watch radio shows. The announcer would come out beforehand and talk in that terribly familiar voice we'd heard a million times, but his face didn't fit the voice we knew at all. He would warm up the audience with some jokes and tell us that when he pointed at us he wanted to hear some clapping. Then the show would begin, and I was always amazed that the magic world that came over my little bedside radio was really only a few ordinary people standing around a microphone holding scripts and reading back and forth. Of course, that wasn't completely true—they showed us the sound effects room afterwards, how thunder was made by shaking a sheet of tin, how a little contraption of wooden sticks made horses' hooves, and what made rain and gun shots and creaking doors and rattling chains and all the spooky noises I loved so well.

Then we would be whisked away to the Museum of Science and Industry, where the wonders of life were all explained: how engines work, the telephone and telegraph, dams, water power, electricity, gravitation, airplanes, everything. There were a thousand things to do there—buttons to push to start wheels or exhibits or put flashing lights in motion or to start toy trains or engines made of glass so you could see their insides working. There were telephones to talk into for ten seconds, then hear what you said played back to see how you sounded to someone else over the phone. The best thing to do was "the smells." You'd push your nose up to a little screen and start pulling levers. The first one might be marked Cinnamon, and the sharp, sweet smell of cinnamon toast would come spurting out and you'd breathe deeply. Next might be Violets or Pineapple or Burning Leaves or Pungent. Whenever I got to the lever marked Putrid, I got scared, I had to force myself to get my nose close up to the smell place and closed my eyes when I pulled, not breathing in quite as hard this time.

My mother kept us moving, and pretty soon she had us out of there and on the way to the next attraction, whether it was a movie at the Trans-Lux or watching the stars move over the great dome universe at the Planetarium, or gazing through the glass Aquarium windows at strange colored fish in a world of water, or eating at the Automat, each of us supplied with ten nickels to drop in the slots of any delicious window we chose. Then it was the circus, if it was that time of year, or Radio City Music Hall, where she took us high up in the balcony to watch the movie on that unbelievably huge screen below, and at the end of the film she would have us up and running down to the main floor, down an aisle, bumping into all the people leaving, getting ahead of all the new people coming in, right to the very first row so we could look straight down into the orchestra pit, watch the musicians taking their seats, turning on the little lights of their music stands, tuning up, calling jokes to one another. We'd catch an eye and wave and the cellist would wave back up. Then the lights would go out and the orchestra would start to rise, silently at first, but when it got almost to our level, the leader would shake his baton for attention and with a great wave he would bring a burst of music out of the musicians. The curtains would rise now and we would be encompassed by a world of dancing legs and flashing costumes.

One of the high points of each year was the night my mother let us stay up as late as we wanted. Usually lights-off was seven thirty, right after gluing our ears to the radio and listening to the latest exploits of Jack, Doc and Reggie in "I Love a Mystery." One summer she combined a staying-up-all-night with a spree and that was best of all.

It was a summer we had a rented house at the Jersey shore. My father came down on the train for weekends. We missed him and waited for him, and looking forward to staying up all night made the waiting easier. It happened during the week when he wasn't there, and we had waited for this night all month, been promised it and finally it came, starting out with hot dogs for dinner at Asbury Park, then a movie —*Earthworm Tractors* starring Joe E. Brown. The theater was right in the amusement park, so when we got out we were suddenly dazzled by the noise and bright lights of the midway. Now we chomped into the pink air of cotton candy and rode the roller coaster half a dozen times, finally getting the back seat in the back car to get the best whip-crack at the end of a dive or on a sharp turn. We groped our way through the spooky house, clutching each other and quaking with fascinated fear as cackling skeletons reached toward us with their bony fingers and fake snakes slithered across our faces. On the merry-go-round we gripped our horses with our knees, held an ear with the left hand, leaned out to the right and made desperate lunges for a ring each time we came around to the ring holder. My sister got a gold one which gave her two free rides. My mother watched from the sidelines as our cries became sirens. Our hearts were beating to the calliope, our blood seemed to race as fast as the coaster itself, rising up to the top of our brains, then plunging, twisting, coursing, lunging, roaring through the steep, deep tunnels of our bodies.

To calm us down my mother took us for a walk on the beach. It was a moonless night and we could only see the rim of roiling white on top of the waves as they reared up their huge black backs before cresting, breaking, slapping in a white thunder onto the packed sand.

Back at the house, my mother told us we looked pretty sleepy already, and here it was just the start of the evening. We said maybe we ought to do the staying up all night business some other night and she said, oh, no, this was the night and for us to have a good time awake because she was tired and was going to sleep now.

It was ten thirty. My brother went into his room and said he would see us at midnight, he had a stack of new Big Little books to read. My sister and I played slap-jack and listened to the radio and after awhile we went in to see my brother and he was asleep. We marked the time—five minutes after eleven. He just couldn't take it. Too young. No stamina. We laughed together at our brother's poor plight, put out the light, covered him and went back to our cards.

"I wonder what dawn on the beach looks like?" I asked.

"We'll know in about six hours," Nancy answered. "We'll go out there and see around five."

But pretty soon she was yawning and my eyelids felt like weights. We went into the bathroom and made cold compresses out of wet washcloths which we held to our foreheads and the backs of our necks to chase away sleep. I lay on my bed, letting the cold work and watching the hands of the Big Ben alarm clock. We were determined to see midnight anyway. When I woke the next morning at eight thirty, I remembered getting to twenty of, and even though my sister claimed she made it to the stroke of twelve, I never have believed her.

Today, thirty-five years later and recently home from the hospital, waiting for the dawn is an altogether different matter. I go to bed early, around seven or eight o'clock. My time is the early morning. I wake at two or three, slept out. I get up in the shivering house, thrust up the heat, weigh myself, rub circulation into my hands, brew a pot of tea, shut myself into my study and begin looking through the contents of my father's desk, putting my files in order, reading notes I have jotted to myself over the years, writing things down that seem interesting or pertinent or true.

Weekends have become like weekdays. I have stopped wearing a watch or looking at a calendar or reading the morning paper or watching the news on television. I am escaping from specific dates and times and avoiding the events that measure them. Often, upon waking, I wonder what day is coming up—a Wednesday? a Sunday? the twenty-third? The seventh? It doesn't matter. The approach of Christmas is my only beacon.

My family puts up with me. I wake when I have slept enough. I write until I am tired of writing. I eat when I am hungry. My schedule doesn't jibe with theirs. I am considered, temporarily, as an odd yet specially privileged, tenderly cared for guest, who will be back again as father and as husband sooner or later.

The dawns are the times I both dread and yearn for. Maybe they are too real and at the same time everything I want. I wished to witness and experience them so badly on those stay-up nights so long ago, yet never made a single one. Now I wonder, sitting at my desk in a bay window facing giant pines, if I want the night to break. The electric lights make mirrors of the windowpanes, with the gleam on the inside of the glass sharpened by the black night outside. I can look at myself staring back in either of the three windows of the bay and I can look into my eyes and see how much weight I have lost off my face.

The large middle window points east. I wait. Then, as the pale light sneaks into the dark sky once more, the past and present seem to come together, life and death seem close, innocence blends with all that I have learned, and with the sun comes hope.

※◇◇※

The Crunch
of Gravel

DURING MY CONVALESCENCE THIS CHRISTMASTIME, I was struck by how much our many family rituals meant to everybody in the house, especially my children. Maybe they were magnified during that time of tension, maybe in that period of uncertainty about my health everybody needed to hold on to their own patterns and habits of life, to go through whatever routines they had built up over the years with even more attention than usual. It made me think back to my childhood again, to our lives on the hill which were made up of a network of little routines and rituals. Weekdays passed slowly, we counted them on our school fingers, all of us gathering in a bunch each morning to wave good-by to my father as he chugged Celeste and then Chowdog and finally Angus backwards out of the garage, made her roar and smoke, then shot down the drive to disappear in the green trees, his hand hurling kisses behind. When we were on vacation from school, my brother and I would be out at the garage before him, tugging up the old door on its ungreased tracks, there for a hug or a touch when he came charging out of the house, and we would run beside the car as it got going for a final slap at the rumble seat or the back fender to see who could have the last tap. In the summer he would be back home when it was still light, to work in his garden till the petals on his roses lost their color, but in early spring and in late fall and all winter long he came home in the dark, and we waited for his headlights and the crunch of gravel his tires made before streaming out to the garage again to hurl ourselves upon him. He took his time getting to the house, checking on his flower beds which ran along the carpenter's shop and along the rabbit cage, or if it were winter and there had been ice or snow, shaking off the stooping load from his box bushes, checking on his bird feed tray, looking out over his garden to the twinkling valley way beyond and breathing slow, deep breaths, for he was happy to be at his home again.

His evening rituals were slow, deliberate. Off with hat about halfway between garage and house, loosen tie if it were summer, up the three porch steps, open screen door, let it bang behind, now the heel of a hand to the dark green wood of the front door which always stuck, the clack of the knocker as it got shaken by the opening of the door, the stamping off of snow on the porch. Open wide now and in and hello to everyone. People coming from all over the house to say hello to him, my mother from the top of the stairs, calling and rushing down, Sophie, our cook, coming out of the kitchen and giving that round, brown smile of hers to wish him good evening, Yo-Yo, our tiny English nurse, rapping hello on an upstairs windowpane, and all of us children, if we hadn't been outside, streaking down the banister backwards and being plucked off at the end and hugged.

Off with the rubbers now, or the arctics, standing over by the tiny hall radiator, a lot of hopping on one foot to get the blasted things off, a pat for Hundy who knew a friend when he saw one and waggled a brown ear against my father's trouser leg. Could be straightening the stuff in the umbrella stand now—the Malacca cane with the gold hand-tip which used to belong to his father, the snake cane, the shillelagh, the crook with a griffin's head for a handle, all my pop guns and our wands and wooden swords and stick-horses and homemade bows and arrows and our clubs and spears and stilts and anything else that was thin and stood straight up and could be rammed into an old Chinese umbrella stand.

Soon his hat joined all the other lids of the house on top of the hall chest. Full feather Indian, ten gallon, helmets for everything from football to jousting, cardboard crown with golden points, slicker, three-cornered, peaked, pirate, coon's tail, stovepipe magic, black hood, leather racer, beanie, visor, tam. We wore them, one one day, one the next, hat-masks to change us into anybody we felt like being, to disguise us from the world, to transform us to anytime, anywhere.

Now open the gorilla closet underneath the stairs. Force coat and hanger onto the packed bar, head disappearing for a moment among all those camphor coats, a sudden pounding against the back of the closet, a growl, jumping back, slamming the door shut and leaning on it. "He almost got me then, that old Egor," my father said, panting fright. We never saw the wild, ferocious gorilla, Egor, that lived back in there somewhere in the closet, but he was surely there—didn't he growl and pound every evening my father disturbed him again?

Open the pipe cabinet now. Shelf upon shelf of pipes—straight stems, curved stems, blackened bowls, one in a leather box the shape of a fat pipe which clicked open and revealed a white meerschaum beauty with a fierce Viking's head for its bowl, lying there in a bed of purple velvet. The sweet aroma of tobacco. Opening a tin of tobacco and dipping the pipe down into the deep mulch, and scooping the tobacco out, pressing and packing it down with the thumb, sucking to see if the packing was just right, whipping a kitchen match underneath a shelf. And the lighting, the popping sound of sucking and drawing, the first crisp burning and the blue smoke and the heavy, rich, sweet, wet smell.

The evening ritual continued. Up the stairs, squeeze left through the tiny, heavily booked back hall, into the bathroom. Unload pockets onto the top of the highboy. Gold pocket watch and chain with gold penknife at the other end. Pennies, nickels, dimes and quarters. Subway tokens. Wallet. Letters of the day. I had to get a chair to see it all—spread out there with the cuff links and the tie clips, the half-gone roll of peppermint Life Savers, the gold pen and pencil, the little black leather date book, the horn-rimmed reading glasses, the folding leather tobacco pouch, the bits of paper and notes and dollar bills and odds and ends and all the other secrets of his business day.

Over to the bathtub. Plug the rubber stopper in, twist handles until the faucets steamed and gushed. A slow, careful undressing, hanging up of coat and vest and pants as it progressed, rid of shirt, underclothes and socks into the green hamper at the foot of the tub. Stepping into the tub now and sitting down, which made the water rise to an inch from overflowing. In we went, too, sometimes, one at a time, sitting at the other end facing him, both cramped and pinched in that tiny tub.

"I'll have a foot," he would say and go for one underwater and catch it and hold it tight and do its sole with the scrubbing brush until we screamed for mercy. The black grub of the day's running would slowly come off and the legs got white and their bruises began to show; and after we had lathered down and dunked and come up like frogs, we hopped out dripping into a warm towel from the radiator, and as we shivered and got rubbed down by my mother, he did the rest of his washing, with a little elbow room now, and finished up by slipping down on his back, going under backwards holding his nose, submerging completely and then suddenly bursting the surface again.

When he was dressed in his khaki shorts and his green

L. L. Bean shirt, we went down through the pantry to the cellar steps. They were steep and worn, and the dirt floor down there with the furnace made the smell moist and earthy. The steel shovel scraped on the cement floor of the coal bin and the blue-black chunks rattled into the scuttle. Through the slits in the door of the little furnace that made the hot water, low blue flames jumped and played. The new cold coal crashed down in a landslide and for a moment seemed to extinguish the fire, but soon little orange licks appeared in the black coal cracks.

Feel the hot water tank, check the pressure. Doddle around a bit. Putter. When we were ready to go up, we each piled ourselves high with firewood from the split cord against the cellar wall. Up the stairs we groaned, through the pantry, dining room, hall—to the fireplace in the living room. He crumpled newspaper, kneeling, broke the kindling, laid the fire with dry pine boughs on top which blew up with the struck match sending white heat and Fourth of July sparklers against the charred bricks and up the black hole of the chimney. I could lie in front of that fire for hours and look into its flames and feel its heat on my face and follow the shadows and flickers it made on the walls. I could listen to the life in the house, to the pad of feet in the bedroom over the living room, the voices, the radio purring in my sister's room above, the new baby's cry, the clicking of dishes from the kitchen, my brother's feet banging down next to my ears as he pretended to jump on my head—catch one of them and send him dumping—the rustling of papers at my father's desk, my mother's needles working on a new sweater for him, Hundy yawning beside us, the wind outside.

That was about it on weekdays—nothing really special at all, yet quite a bit special, quite a lot to be remembered. On weekends there was even more.

There was working with my father in the garden or playing a game of tackle with him or swimming or helping with the bees or the fig tree or snow shoveling, or skiing with him, sledding, bushwhacking, chopping. It could be a fishing trip to Black River, which meant getting up at five o'clock Saturday morning and cracking eggs in a glass, shaking in salt and pepper, and quaffing it all down raw for nourishment. It could be having a bit of home hokum with our collection of rubber masks. He'd slip on a monster mask over his head with an ugly scar drooling down the cheek and I'd be a werewolf, and we'd creep up through the box bushes and claw at a window to scare somebody half to death in the living room. And we might even go so far as to get the proper people on the second floor, too, by putting a glove on a long stick and making it go rap rap against the windowpane.

On Saturday night my father might let my brother and me and a friend or two go camping far back on the other side of the hill. We would pack up our tent and blankets and food and equipment and say good-by and hike to the spot between two big pines where the ground was a soft mattress of winter-brown needles and the trunks perfect for tying up pup tent ropes.

We would pitch camp, cook supper, clean up, get in our tents when the dark came, and we'd be fixing the mosquito netting and telling each other scary stories when out of the black came a breaking of twigs and a deep, low bear's growl. Our hearts stopped. We froze. Someone finally got the courage to shine the flashlight out of the mouth of the tent to see what was there. Another growl. Some more twigs breaking. The brave one aimed the beam of light right at the growl. There, on all fours, was my father. He was making a bear's face and getting ready to make his third growl. He smiled and stood up, but he was a little disappointed he had been uncovered so soon. We told him to stop being so funny. We told him he'd promised to treat us like big boys and leave us all by ourselves the whole night. But he never could resist checking up, just to make sure the fire was out and everything was all right with us.

Sunday morning was getting ready for Sunday dinner. The smell of the roast filled the house and the white linen tablecloth was laid as soon as the breakfast dishes were cleared. My mother drove us into town to get the fat Sunday newspapers and the ice cream. We called out the flavors and hiked ourselves up onto the counter to see the man dig into the vats with his flat scoop and pack our quart cartons full of yellow vanilla and dark chocolate and tan coffee and speckled green pistachio and red-pink strawberry. On the way home, if we weren't reading the funny papers, someone would sneak a piece of dry ice out of the ice cream jiffy bag, call "think fast," and toss it at his brother. Then a juggling act ensued—hold the white, gassy chunk just a moment too long and a hand would get burned. When we got home, into my father's huge water glass would go the dry ice, making a volcano of bubbles and smoke to startle him when he came in to carve.

After my mother and father had finished their glasses of sherry in the living room, Sophie came to the door and rapped on the wall with her knuckles for attention. Licking her lips and smiling, she said, very formally, imitating a very formal servant in a very formal house, "Dinner is served." My father would say, "Thank you, Sophie," and we'd all stop whatever we were doing and troop into the dining room for Sunday dinner.

My brother and I would race to see who got to pull our mother's chair, and whoever lost whipped around and did it for our father. We shoved them in and then slid into our usual places and our father would start sharpening up the carving knife, holding it by its bone handle and whipping the sharpener across one side of the blade, then the other. My mother would pick up a little silver bell and ring it, and at the tinkle Sophie would push the door to the pantry open with her hip and appear carrying a big silver platter which held upon its gravy-tree base whatever roast we were having that day.

"Couldn't you cut bigger portions, dear?" the conversation might start, my mother telling my father how to do his job. "I know the boys could eat a lot more than those tiny bitty slices you're giving them."

A glare across the table from my father.

From me, "That's exactly the amount I want. Not a sliver more. Not an ounce."

From my brother, "Me, too."

"The boys are just trying to be polite," is my mother's retort. "I really think you ought to cut them more."

To change the subject my brother pipes up, "Guess who I saw yesterday?"

"Who?" asks Nancy.

"Everybody I saw."

A lot of heehaw laughter.

We have our plates with the meat and Sophie is passing the vegetables in their silver dishes, to go along with the mashed potatoes and gravy and jelly and salad and sauces.

"I wish I had teeth in my stomach," is my brother's next offering. "Then I could swallow and just have all the work done for me."

Me sniffing the potatoes. "Oh, how I love potato smoke!"

My father starts telling about the island in Maine he's taking us to this summer.

"There are blueberries," he starts out, "blueberries everywhere, everywhere you look. And if it's still there, there's a fishhawk's nest on top of a buoy, at least it was there when

I visited the island when I was in school; I hope he's still there, keen old fella, that fishhawk. He sails around looking for food and then he shoots down like a stone. I hope you're all going to like clambakes and swimming in that icy water. There are seals up there, I hope we see some, and the mist sifting over the trees. Oh, how I love that place."

"Where do we leave Chowdog if we go to the island?" one of us asks.

"There's a garage on the mainland, we'll leave her there. I hope she won't mind resting in that garage for two weeks. I hope nobody scratches her."

"They can't scratch Chowdog, Daddy," someone chimes in, "don't you remember there's no paint on her. Scratching means there's something to be scratched, so Chowdog's safe."

Nancy speaks. She is remembering our father's Model A. "Dad, you know I really miss Celeste. She was your best car, I think. I liked the holes in the seat. I liked how the steering wheel was covered with a black dampness that came out of the wood and stained your hands every day. I liked how the gas meter always registered zero and you always had to figure how many miles you had gone before filling it up. Best of all I liked the rumble seat and the fungus growing on the inside of her top."

My father, "You're right, Tweets. It wasn't every car by any means that had a fungus growing out of its roof. I got quite attached to that fungus."

My mother: "How silly, though, when the holes got so big in Celeste's roof and so much rain came in that you had to order a new roof, how silly that you made the garage man absolutely definitely promise you that he would leave the fungus growing there and just build the material around it."

I switch to a new topic. "Dad, answer me this one. If gold is where you find it, then where is silver?"

Nobody knew.

"Under the Lone Ranger."

"That's a good one," says Dad. "Did you think of that yourself, son?"

I hadn't, but before I knew it, "Yes" just slipped out.

"Hey, that's a lie," says Ken. "I remember that now, it was in *Boy's Life* at the bottom of the page. Think of it himself! He did not!"

I begin to get red in the face and stare at my plate. My father tries to save me. "We hear things sometimes and they stay in the backs of our minds. It's awfully difficult to know whether one has thought a thought oneself or found it somewhere. We have to be careful about that."

Halfway through the meal my father will probably have slipped off his moccasins underneath the table and he'll be twiddling his bare toes; if my mother spots that she will say in her fake-mad voice, the same voice she uses when she catches him making faces through the car window at drivers who are annoying him, "Really, this has gone a little too far. What will Sophie think?" And my father will say he's sorry, he'll put on his shoes again if he must, but since he has to wear a hot suit and heavy shoes around the city all week long, he thought bare feet would be all right on the weekends. And my mother will relent since she knows Sophie is perfectly used to Dad by now.

About dessert time—ice cream and cake and more milk to wash everything down—Edith toddles in, just picked up from her nap by Yo-Yo. She tells about how she has been bitten by a wasp in the attic that morning. She shows us the Band-aid that is curing her foot.

"Oh, I'm so sorry," says Dad. "Did it have big wings?"

"Big wings, Daddy."

"How many legs did it have? Did it have two legs?"

"Two legs, Daddy."

"Did it have ten legs?"

"Ten legs, Daddy."

"Did it have black fur on its back?"

"Black fur."

"Did it growl... *grrrrrr!*"

Now Edith catches on that her father is joking with her and she is so delighted she runs across the floor and hugs his leg.

"Yes, it growled, Daddy, *grrrrrrr!*" And she and Dad growl together and laugh and growl to their hearts' content.

That was Sunday dinner.

Afterwards we'd go outside to work the food off, to the garden, to the wood splitting place, to the burning spot, to the snow forts or the tree house, or to walk all over the hill, back to the graveyard on the far side, to the sled run or the quince trees, along the paths, bushwhacking now, slicing our way along the hill until the skies grew red and our stomachs were flat and empty again and darkness was coming.

Sunday evening was reserved for "Pappy's Own." That was a salad for men only. It was called Pappy's Own because my father had invented it, but my brother and I had named it, and for years, although he probably would have liked to eat something different once in a while on Sunday night, we wouldn't let him.

The women, still glutted from the noon feast, nibbled at shredded wheat or milk toast or went to their rooms with nothing at all to eat. My brother and my father and I took over the kitchen. The huge salad bowl, hewn out of a trunk of a great tree, lived on the pantry table just behind the lazy Susan. The turntable was always so full of grinders and shakers and jars and bowls, preserves, sugars, mustards and relish, silver bells and candy and spices and syrups—maybe yesterday's mail as well—it swayed and groaned when spun, and usually some of its load had tumbled off into the salad bowl, the wood of which glistened with years of olive oil sheen. We'd pluck out whatever lazy-Susan stuff was in there by mistake, along with the fruit and raisins and nuts and nutcrackers and napkins which might be there legitimately, and we'd carry the bowl into the kitchen, holding it in our arms like a cradle, and with great ceremony we'd place it in the middle of the white enamel kitchen table. That was the first step for Pappy's Own.

The second step was the flushing out of anything edible from the icebox. Roast bones came first. The last vestiges of meat were cut and scraped and torn off those bones now and thrown into the salad bowl and then the carcasses, be they chicken or turkey, cow, lamb or pig, were all stuffed together into a great pot, covered with water and herbs and sloshed onto the back burner of the coal stove to simmer overnight and make soup for the week.

Now, into the salad bowl went every other leftover —every potato, every vegetable. There might be twelve garden varieties heaved in there. A head of lettuce was torn up and thrown in. A half dozen tomatoes cut in wedges and tossed in. Oil and vinegar and salt and pepper and mustard powder and a dash of sugar. With heavy wooden claws we stirred and tossed the mess and then the three of us sat around the kitchen table and ate it right out of the bowl. There was a lot of smacking of lips and sighs of delight and congratulations for the dressing.

Then the washing took place. All the dishes from lunch had been left, for Sophie had Sunday afternoon and evening off. They were piled high in the sink with their gravy and their ice cream drying on their faces. I fought my father for the wash position. Who liked to dry and put away and swab off the dining room table?—they were secondary jobs. The one back of the sink was the leader. He set the pace and called the shots. When my father was doing it, the pace was careful and deliberate and things really got washed well, but slowly. Whenever I managed to beat him to it—and that always took some fast footwork at the end of Pappy's Own and a little wrestling, too—then the pace picked up, for I was more like a circus performer than a dishwasher. I liked to be dramatic about the thing, going at it like crazy with a lot of show and movement and pizzazz, filling the sink with a mountain of hot suds, scraping and sloshing the food off the plates with fancy handwork, juggling all the stuff with a great flying of hands as each plate and glass, fork, spoon and knife got presto cleaned, rinsed, stacked in the rack on the worn, grooved wood of the sink board, ready for a pair of drying hands and a towel to whip them away, work them over and pile them still warm in their closets and drawers—all amid a shower of singing and wild jokes and water. In the middle of the procedure I had to change the sink water for the final pots and pans that had been sitting sizzling on the burners of the coal stove, softening the food in them.

There was so much sloshing and overflowing and dripping that, at the end, when the sink water was going out with a gurgle and a choke, the washer had to mop the floor up. He also was in charge of filling the stove with water while somebody else shook down the ashes, shoveled them out into a little bucket and filled the stove with coal from a scuttle. This particular stove had a tank in it that gave us instant boiling water from a tap in front. You filled the tank by holding a short piece of hose onto the nozzle of the sink faucet and then, with a big stretch, holding the other end of the hose over the top of the open hot water tank behind one of the stove's burners. The washer also got to wind the big clock over the sink, which was the last part of the Sunday night ritual.

He Could Not Hold on to Everything

THE DESK AGAIN.

It is hard not to return to it. This time it helps make the point that nothing in our house ever got thrown away. My father's desk was always piled high and the drawers packed so tight he could hardly wrench them open to add something more. But he had a natural sense of order to him, and often, on a rainy weekend afternoon, he sat down to clean it up, get rid of some of that stuff.

Even though the desk was in the back living room, it was a private piece of furniture, untouchable to us. My father did his work there, wrote his letters, mostly using it in the evenings after dinner with Hundy lying close by and some Mozart playing on his Victrola in the corner of the room. He wrote hundreds of letters each year, to us away at boarding school, to all the members of his family and my mother's family on their birthdays, and to his friends on their anniversaries or birthdays, and even to a lot of members of my generation, his nephews and nieces and godchildren and just plain friends of mine or my sisters and brothers whom he

liked particularly and whom he wanted to know he felt
something special about them. He was like a second father
to my friends because he always seemed to have time for
them. He talked to them directly, remembering every little
detail about them, and some of them brought problems to
him to discuss, and he treated them like his own children,
giving them the same kind of time and advice he always
gave us.

Often he was so tired at night after working over bills
and business matters that his head nodded, but before leaving
his desk he would always look into his miniature black
leather diary-calendar which had the list of birthdays he
wanted to remember, and if there was one coming up, he
would force a letter out of himself. If one of his own children was coming home late, from a party, from school or
college, or leaving the house earlier in the morning than he
for some reason, our father would never fail to write an
affectionate note to us, welcoming us, hoping that we had
had fun at anything we might have been doing, saying that
he couldn't wait to see us in the morning but don't get up,
sleep late, and he would make himself wait for that pleasure
until he got home the following evening, or saying good-by
and what fun it had been to see us and wishing us well and
sending us his love. These notes, written out on long sheets
of yellow paper, we found pinned to the front door, or lying
on the front stairs, or shoved underneath the doors of our
rooms.

He wrote his important letters slowly and carefully, making a first draft, crossing out things he thought were expressed badly, writing in over the cross-outs. When he was pleased with a letter, he would copy it over in his perfectly spaced, beautifully arched handwriting. If it was a letter having to do with a big decision on his part, or a letter that was going to mean a great deal to the person who was getting it, he would show the first draft to my mother, who would very gently do any fixing there had to be done. A few times he would ask her to write down suggestions or an outline of what he might say, and she would write it as if he were talking, not she; for in those young years he felt he was inarticulate and not sophisticated enough, but she always built him up, made him think that he had done it all, that they were all his words and his ideas from the beginning. Actually his letters were not inarticulate at all. If he were writing to a person he liked, his affection for that person came through direct and strong—he just said what he felt about them.

Back to the cleaning up of the desk. He would sit there with a wastepaper basket at his feet and he would start going over everything on top of the desk first, his briefcase full of work from the office, the current mail, bills, receipts. Not much there he could throw away, except for some used envelopes, so how about the drawers? He would pull them out one by one and go through them slowly, but never with much luck. There might be a scrap here, a form letter there, or an ad or something else inconsequential that had somehow snuck in. But he did not have the heart to heave out all the letters from his friends congratulating him on his engagement, and then his marriage, or all the letters and notes and cards my mother had ever written him, or all the communications from us, however crude the drawings and the messages were in the beginning. And who would have wanted to throw away the hospital receipts for the births of his children, or the receipt from the van company that moved all my mother's and father's worldly possessions from New York City to the hill for one hundred and ten dollars, a year after they were married; or the letters of sympathy to him at his father's death, and then at his mother's; or the correspondence with Arthur Riddlesdale Powne-Dammit, Late Curate of Bath, to Sir Egbert Bobleigh, Part-Wapping, Lower Barton—those were the names my father's roommate at college and he used when writing each other.

Exactly how expendable were the letters to and from the nursery from which he ordered his roses; or the correspondence with the company that sold him his bee equipment; with the oil company that started selling him oil for his new burner at six and one-half cents a gallon a few years after he moved to the hill, when it replaced the coal furnace; or the letter from the Department of Agriculture giving him its recommendations for spraying for Japanese beetles; or the $426 estimate for building the two new little rooms on the side of our house when Edith was born; or the application for registration to the American Kennel Club—filled out but never sent in—that came with Hundy when my father's brother gave him to us (who could believe plain old Hundy was sired by Harbor Hill, AKC No. 815337, and the dam—Penelope II—AKC No. 756499?); or the letter from the motor company about our new car, telling him they would allow $250 on the old one and that would mean we could have a brand new DeLuxe Fordor with radio and heater for $621; or all those instruction sheets and pamphlets that mounted up in one of the drawers, instructions for the underwater flashlight and for the nonglare desk lamp, instructions for a box model DeWald radio, for a balsa wood model of the *China Clipper*, for a magic set, a disguise kit, a Lionel catalog whose back page showed a picture of a plane that "loops and stunts by remote control—$10.95"; or all our report cards; or, to go way back, to the very bottom and back of one of the drawers, all those diaries he had kept when he had been in school, all the quotes about nature and about life by Emerson and Thoreau and Shakespeare and many others that he had written out so that they would not just disappear after a school course—he would have them with him always.

So the cleaning out was more a taking out and rearranging and putting back in again affair. It was the same all over the house—nobody could ever bear to part with hardly anything at all. When our clothes were outgrown or worn or when blankets got holes in them or when games or toys got tattered or tiresome, or schoolbooks got obsolete or when another box got filled with letters, up they'd all go to the attic to be packed away in chests and steamer trunks and boxes and left to stew there under the eaves.

The cellar was used the same way. It was too damp for clothes, but it got every magazine that ever came into the house, a good percentage of the newspapers, old jars and pots and worn-out kitchen equipment, broken skis and bicycles that had had their front wheels run over.

The other two floors of the house weren't much better off because my mother was always acquiring huge stacks of old books. Her interest, inherited from her father who was a pioneer collector of early American photographs, was the Civil War and especially Abraham Lincoln and everything about his times. She would go two and three times a week to a secondhand book shop in town which got very good collections from the libraries of the big old houses all over the East, and each time she would come home with at least half a dozen books, and sometimes the whole back seat of the car would be full of them. The library downstairs, which was also the back living room, was already full, so first of all a lot of old standing bookcases were bought and placed along the walls of the back hall; when they were full, additional stacks of books were piled on top until they reached the ceiling, and other stacks on the floor in front of the cases soon grew, so that pretty soon it was worth your life to use that hallway. First of all you had to turn sideways and suck gut to get through at all, but the danger was that if you happened to hit a key book with an elbow, you might get a landslide of a ton of them on your head.

When the back hall was full, then books started to wander up to the front hall and pretty soon my mother's clothes closet was full of books, and then my father's, and finally even the space between the two closets, the space in front of the window that used to give us all such a nice view of the garden before it got its book barrier. Soon they began to creep into my father's and mother's bedroom, too, in great stacks against the wall, in swiveling bookshelves, then underneath the beds, finally even on top. For that was where my mother did a lot of her researching and reading and note-taking and work. She would sit on her own bed and she would lay out the books she wanted to read and to refer to on my father's bed, and by the end of the day his bed had at least a foot deep of books and notes spread over it. When he got home, he would make jokes about Mr. Lincoln being in his bed, and she would take the books off and make a swaying skyscraper of them in the last open corner of the room, but they were back on his bed again the next morning as soon as he was out of it.

My mother didn't stop with books for her researching. She doted on strange and fascinating and minuscule information of all kinds. She drove with the garbage man in his truck to see how delicious garbage was and to find out exactly what he thought about the garbage and how he could tell whose garbage it was without even looking at the house it came from, just by inspecting what was in the cans. She sat in the barber shop for hours to see all the things Mr. DeFalco did to people's hair. She went to farms and zoos and studied each animal, how they looked and walked and ate and licked themselves and how they used their tails and ears.

The amount of paper that was used in our house was extraordinary, first of all because my mother was constantly taking notes on all these things for her children's books, plus notes on every member of the family, what he or she was like, what they said, what they did, over the years. And we children were all doing a lot of paper work, too—drawing pictures, making valentines and cards for every special occasion, writing stories, inking out rules for the Wolf Pack (that was my gang), and for a few years I was putting out my own private family paper on the little printing press I got for Christmas. It was *The P.K. Paper*, filled with family news. Flash extras came out about three or four times a day on weekends with headlines telling about Hundy's cut paw, or that my grandparents had just called to say they were driving out for Sunday lunch, or that the nest of bees in the garage wall was swarming and my father was trying to attach a "bee escape" to the hole in the wall where they lived and catch them for his hives. There were less hot news items, too, social notes about the household, who had done what to whom lately, a lost and found section, latest jokes, overheard remarks, classifieds for anyone in the family who had a message for anyone else, editorials proposing such things as put up or shut up from brothers and three-day weekends for fathers.

And do you have the slightest suspicion that any of this stuff of ours ever got thrown out? Of course it didn't. It got purloined by my mother and filed away in big department store boxes that suits or coats had come in, a stack of which was forever growing in her work closet in the attic.

It was the same in my mother's and father's bathroom. This was a good meeting place for the whole family, for it opened out into the back hall so we could get in easily and it also opened into their bedroom. We gathered there when my father was shaving, standing naked in front of the little white sink and shaving into a medicine chest mirror. Blops of soap and beard dropped into the hot water as he scraped away, holding an ear out of the way when he got to it, bending up the lobe, and when he was ready for the upper lip, he would stick his tongue in underneath it and make it bulge out so that the shaving was easier. When he was finished, he would run his fingers over his slippery cheeks to see if he had missed a bristle, and then he pulled the plug and there was a whirlpool sucking gurgle leaving a sandstorm of beard-flakes all over the porcelain sides which he washed away with his hand and a squirt of cold water. We gathered there to watch him take his polar bear baths during the months ice kept him from having his morning swim in the pool. He'd swim every morning right up to the first skim of ice; then, for the winter months, he'd trade that way of cooling off the blood for ice-cold tubs which made even him gasp as he sat down fast and went under and came up panting and pink-skinned.

Over the claw-foot bathtub, cracks in the light-green plaster wall ran like rivers on a map. Along that wall was a long, high open shelf of tubes and jars and boxes and bottles, of vials and rolls and brushes and pads. There and in a high, many-shelved closet was a gaggle of medicines and equipment. It grew and grew over the years because no bottle or box was ever chucked unless it was completely empty, drained to the last drop or grain, and that hardly ever happened. There was brown Pertussin for coughs and blue and white half-empty bottles of Milk of Magnesia, crusting at the caps. There were toothbrushes and aspirin and eau de cologne, asthma powder, enema bags and mustard for plasters. There were atomizers and hot-water bottles and a steamer for benzoin. Oil of citronella there was and insect repellant and boxes of face powder with their chalky puffs. There was albumin and boric acid, tooth powder, honey and almond lotion, Sal Hepatica, salt, a pumice stone, sunburn oil, baking soda, Stokes Expectorant, eye cups, paragoric, sponges, lamb's wool, rolls of bandages, combs and hairbrushes, iodine, mercurochrome, soaps, resin, cold cream, cotton, sulfa powder, razor blades, calamine, tape and Vaseline, shampoo, rubbing alcohol, castor oil, Alka-seltzer, nose drops, nail polish, salt tablets, soda mints, gold paint, scissors,

and clippers and Kaopectate and mouthwash and old pre-
scriptions by the score, even one bottle which gave no more
information than "one tablespoon every hour until effec-
tive."

Beside the medicine cabinet was a narrow closet where
my father's suits hung. His shoes and sneakers and slippers
were on the floor of the closet and on a shelf up high, way
over in the right-hand corner where nobody but he could
get at it, was a pistol. He kept it for the crows. In the summer they would come every morning at five thirty, sit in the
limbs of the horse chestnut tree just outside his window and
try to wake him up with their loud hawking voices. At first
he would stalk into the bathroom, mumbling and cursing,
and get out the gun. He would take some bullets off the
shelf, too, and load the clip that fitted into the handle. And
then he would very gently edge open the bathroom window
that faced the horse chestnut tree and he would get down
on one knee and take aim out into the murk of dawn. A sudden crack as the shot was fired! The crows all took off from
their perches in a dither, cawing and flapping away at a
great rate, laughing, I think, probably giggling and laughing,
practically in hysterics, because none of them ever got hit.
But the laugh was really on them, for I can't believe he really
ever aimed for one.

Maybe once every few years my father made a valiant
effort to get rid of a hunk of the ever-growing mountain in
the cellar and attic. He would carry armfuls of it down the

narrow attic steps, squeeze past the books in the back hall, down the kitchen stairs and then out the back door to his burning place. Or he would lug a pile up the cellar stairs and trudge it around to the fire. That fire would burn all afternoon. My mother gave strict orders which magazines and newspapers could go, which couldn't. They were the first to burn, that was easy, but whenever he came to something that was really connected to some member of his family, he would pause. It could be a little stuffed monkey that I had been given when I was one, the yellow gauzy skin all faded now, the straw insides sticking out of holes gnawed by squirrels, the button eyes long gone and the head dangling over a shoulder. He would hold the monkey in his hand for some time, thinking back about it, puffing on his pipe as the trees stirred in the late afternoon breeze, remembering. He might have even bent toward the fire with it once, realizing that he could not hold on to everything. But he could not do it, and finally he would set the monkey up in a crotch of a tree, prop it up there so it could watch him during the rest of the burning.

By the end of the day it seemed that half of the stuff he had set out to burn was sitting up in that tree—a ragged brown sweater that my brother had worn for years, sticks we had fashioned into horses and ridden over the hill until they frothed at the mouth and neighed for oats and rest, all kinds of costumes we had made with flowing cloaks and cardboard armor painted silver—doublets, dagger belts, swords whittled out of sticks, mail stockings of crocheted string, masks, and hats of every kind and helmets. Up there in the tree alongside the monkey went a whole zoo of stuffed animals we used to take to bed.

So at end of the day when the fire had died to embers and was glowing a deep red in the oncoming dark, my father would gather up everything from the tree in his arms, all those animals and costumes, a wool hat of my brother's that reminded him of a long-ago winter, a tiny shirt of my sister's, and he would carry them all back into the kitchen, up the two flights of stairs to the attic and carefully pack them away again.

<hr />

Christmas

A FEW YEARS AFTER WE WERE MARRIED KATHARINE and I moved to Los Angeles, and, for the six years we lived there, the poor postmen were almost driven crazy at Christmastime. Everybody in our families back East sent presents to us, and our children, everybody from grandfathers and grandmothers right on down to little cousins. A package might even come with the address written in disguised writing as if a baby had scribbled it. You might even get a present from your old dog you left back home on the hill. So all that meant something like one hundred packages of various lengths, widths, weights, colors, textures, shapes, arriving: make that five hundred, because there were five of us out there in California, we had three children already. Of course, the packages usually arrived air mail special delivery or special handling, or something else special the postman had to do, half of them coming the last forty-eight hours before Christmas, because things seldom got done tidily in advance by a lot of members of my family back home.

But there was one very special package that always arrived on time each year, just a week before Christmas. It was the oddest-shaped, most carefully wrapped, most perfectly signed and sealed package we got all December. Katharine and our children and I waited for it as Christmas approached, knowing that it would come and that the postman would arrive staggering up our steps with the same strange look in his eye that he had fixed us with the year before. We would take the package from him, sign the necessary papers, thank him a lot and get rid of him fast, get the thing in quickly because we were always scared somebody might make a slip and admit the nature of the contents, laying us open for confiscation, for what was inside was surely breaking California's plant and bug law and making an illegal entry into the state.

The postman wouldn't have believed what was inside the package anyway, because who would send something through the mails that was worth practically nothing with at least ten dollars' worth of postage stamps smacked all over the package? The package was makeshift—fashioned out of cardboard from several different cartons taped together and joined with rolls and rolls of brown wrapping paper and two-inch wide, lick-it-and-die brown tape. My mother, who is the most expert and extravagant wrapper and signer and sender of all times, was responsible for the packing, and she wrote our name and address in huge black India ink letters at least three or four times on different areas of the thing she had created, along with a great many special instructions like *Rush* or *Fragile* or *Deliver Immediately* or *Handle with Loving Care,* all with exclamation marks after each exhortation. It wasn't all that easy to get the thing open. It took knives and scissors and ripping, but we finally got all that brown paper and cardboard off, and inside was a giant plastic bag which we ripped off, too, and there it was—a Christmas tree from the hill.

Wrapped and wadded around the stump were washcloths and towels which had been soaked in water to give the tree a drink on its trip out and keep it fresh. Its branches were all tied up around its trunk to make it as thin as possible for mailing, but when the string got cut, the branches began to sink right down again. We stood the tree in a bucket of water overnight. The next day we put it up beside a window and decorated it with some of the old tinsel and bells that my father and mother had sent out, too—wrapped in cotton so the delicate colored glass of the bells and balls would not get crushed by the postal system. I would hoist up a child on my shoulders to hang the same star we'd always hung on our trees back there on the hill—they'd sent that out as well. And I would try to visualize my father and my sister Edith, who was in her teens now, going out in the snow for a walk over the hill to find the perfect tree to send to California.

That's how Christmas on the hill always used to start for us, the searching and the finding and the cutting of the tree. We'd do it a week or ten days before Christmas itself, usually on a Sunday afternoon. My father would get his tree-saw from its nail on the cellar wall—the saw was as tall as I was with a fierce row of inch-high teeth—and we'd gather outside for my mother to tell us from the dining room window to be sure to find a perfect one, bushy on all sides and especially at the base, no holes in it, no imperfections, with a perfect point for the star.

We walked down the road toward the sheep barn, past the path to the pool, past the sliding hill, and we turned sharp right up an old, overgrown evergreen road in the woods. After some climbing we hit the back part of the Ring Road —that was where the best trees were on the hill. There was a whole slope of them along a ridge where George Washington's soldiers had camped one winter a century and a half ago. In the earth among the new trees there were still the squares of leveled earth where the soldiers of Brigadier General John Stark's Brigade had built their huts on the steep hillside. Two Connecticut regiments, one from Massachusetts and Colonel Israel Angell's Rhode Islanders shivered out the winter of 1780 there, drank from our spring, paraded on our fields, could see from their perch on our hill the flaming tar barrel fifteen miles east which was the alarm signal that the British were on the move west from Staten Island.

There were a few giant pines on the hillside that might have been already standing in Stark's day, but between them, scattered all about, were trees the size we were after, and we stomped through the snow, circling each one that caught an eye to get a 360-degree view of it. My father's yardstick for our tree's height was his six feet plus an upstretched arm and hand, then add another stretched hand, little finger to thumb—all together that was the distance between the floor and ceiling in our living room.

"This one, this is it," my sister would call. "It's perfect!"

And my father would stride over and start working his measuring device on it.

"It's top is lousy," my brother would point out fast, "it's all shabby up there. It doesn't come to a good point."

"It has a chunk out of the other side," I would add.

Everybody wanted to be the one who found the chosen tree.

My father rubbed his chin. He ventured that it might be hard to hang a star on a top that went three ways aslant instead of one straight up. My sister had already given up on that one and had another tree picked out down the hill. My brother was calling "Perfect! Perfect!" from higher up. But, of course, I had spotted the only really truly magnificently one hundred percent perfection tree, except no matter how hard I called about it, my father didn't seem to hear. He was stomping around in the snow almost in a trance, not really paying any attention to his midget tree-screamers at all, measuring all the time with his eye, reaching in among branches and taking hold of trunks and shaking so that snow would fall off and he could see a specimen without its white disguise.

"Don't you think this is a beauty?" he would say.

"I spied that one three hours ago," my brother said.

"You're a liar. You never saw it before in your life. You stink anyway," I was quick to tell him.

From somewhere through the pine and snow, my sister added something insulting about neither of us having the brains to spot anything beautiful anyway. We all congregated around the tree in question, circling it again and again, trying to pick holes in it, but when it came right down to business, there weren't any holes to pick, it was a beauty all right, it was OK, yes, it was our tree.

We all agreed. My father got down on his knees, pushed branches aside, and laid the teeth of the great saw against the trunk, right above the snow line. He began to cut, slowly and straightly across, so that the base would be flat and even. We all held different parts of the tree so that finally, after a few forward and backward thrusts and slices of the saw, when the tree base was severed, it didn't fall over and snap a branch off.

My father stood up and dusted the snow patches from his knees and took the end of the trunk and we lowered it on its side and I took the saw and he dragged the tree up the hill to the Ring Road and along it, then down the overgrown old road to our drive and up toward the house, the tree skidding along the snow behind him and us skipping and yelping all about him. There was my mother pulling up the window again and saying, "What a nice tree you found." My father stood it up for her so she could see how it was going to look in the living room. He proudly turned it all the way around to show it had no unsightly holes in it and that its lower branches were thick. My mother said, "Wait, please, I've got to have a picture," and clamped close the window and disappeared to find her camera. Pretty soon she was out with her black box and made us all stand around the tree, holding it up perfectly straight, smiling and showing the saw that had done the cutting, but most important to her, showing ourselves. She snapped a few times and turned knobs and rolled film and looked through sites and snapped some more until my father got impatient and said that was that, it was getting dark and there was still a lot to do about the tree.

We tugged it inside. The branches got squeezed by the sides of the front door, but we edged it through slowly and they didn't break, they popped out again inside the front hall. We dragged it through the living room, leaving a trail of needles and leaves and snow behind on the brown carpet, and in the back living room, just to the left of my father's desk, we set it up, my father lifting it into a heavy cement stand that lived all the rest of the year by the woodpile in the cellar, my brother and I crawling in on our bellies to chock the trunk so it would stand straight, my sister getting a pitcher of water and crawling in, too, filling the trough of the stand so the tree could stay alive for a long while and not shed, my mother going upstairs to the linen closet for a sheet and bringing it down and my father arranging the sheet around the stand to cover it up and make it look as if the tree was still standing in snow. It was just the right height. The top missed the ceiling by an inch. A few dead oak leaves were scattered through the branches, dropped there in the autumn. We left them, part of the decoration.

Now, the trimming. My father got the boxes of decorations out of the chest in the hall. We didn't use lights. They were for commercial trees in town or other people's trees, not for us, because, we were told, a string of lights was a terrible fire hazard. The first thing we put on the tree was the silver tinsel. We started at the bottom and wound it round and round, slowly getting higher, until the whole green tree was wreathed in silver, the tinsel running through the branches, in and out around the trunk like flashing arteries.

It was the practice in our house not to buy any new decorations for our tree. We had boxes of delicate colored bells and balls handed down through the family and we had the tinsel and then some colored paper chains my brother and my sister and I had made, and a gold fish with a pointed nose and some wooden angels. The big gold and silver and red balls went on the bottom, and my father was always very particular about crawling under the tree and hanging a lot of them in the back, on the low branches that faced the book shelves and the wall, so that they would hardly be seen at all, but little bits and flecks of their color would suddenly shine through from far back and give a glint. He thought that was very important.

We handled the ornaments with great care; some of them were so thin and fragile and delicate that a little squeeze would have turned them to powder. They were figures of Santa Claus and the Christ child, and a little yellow glass church bell with a tiny glass clapper that actually tinkled. There were angels and wise men and a whole box of twelve pure silver globes. There were twisted colored icicles and glass snow crystals and sheep and birds of colored glass to hang and dangle from our branches. Around and around the tinsel went. On went the ornaments.

"There's a hole up there." My mother would stand back, eyeing the procedure, and say, "Not a thing in it. A great big gap." And six hands would fly up with hooks and bells and in a twinkling the situation was remedied.

Finally it was finished and nothing remained but the star. It was dark outside now and my father had lit the fire in the fireplace. A white department store box that had brought a Christmas sweater years before was used to house the star. "Tweets," my father said to my sister, "that really is a beautiful star you made. A beauty." She had made it years before, cutting a star shape from a laundry shirt cardboard and pasting on silver paper and then rimming all five points with silver tinsel. It had a loop of tinsel coming off the back for hanging. "Ready?" my father asked, squatting down on his haunches so that my sister could scramble up on his back and sit on his shoulders with her feet dangling down his chest. He stood up and my mother handed the star to my sister. We held our breaths. My father edged close to the tree, leaning right into the branches, right among all the tinsel and bells, holding her legs against his chest and stiffening his neck to keep my sister from falling off in her great lean forward to hang the star on the very top spire of the tree.

"A little to the left," my mother would direct. "It needs to be a little to the left." My sister would lean again, and down beneath her my father would grunt a bit, and a little to the left it would go, and my mother would say "Perfect!" My father would back away from the tree and let my sister down slowly and we'd all stand there and look at the completed tree, all the leaves and branches and tinsel and bells and balls, all the color and flashing glass and coiled paper chains, the whole thing topped off with that silver star, and we'd all agree with my father's judgment—"It's a beauty! A real beauty!"

From the moment the tree was picked and cut and put up in the living room and trimmed and starred, Christmas was in the house for keeps. You couldn't get it out of your head for a second. Your heart beat faster than usual all the time and there was a streak of excitement in you right up the stomach to your throat. School was out and my mother was spending the days in town shopping, and when the car came home, sometimes we were made to hide our eyes or promise to stay in our rooms while certain things too big to wrap or with obvious shapes even with wrapping on them were sneaked out of the car to hiding places in the attic or the cellar, both of which were out of bounds to us at Christmastime.

The house was filled with Christmas carols. Nancy thought she knew how to play the piano, so we listened over and over again to "The First Noel" and "O Little Town of Bethlehem." She played "Silent Night" slowly, just as it should be played, and anybody around at the time would sing along with her—"All is calm, all is bright." On the mantelpiece was a manger with a Christ child in it and a Joseph and a Mary and the three wise men and all the animals, and we sang very slowly, "Away in a manger, no crib for his bed, the little Lord Jesus lay down his sweet head," but we speeded things up with "Hark, the Herald Angels Sing" and we decked the halls with boughs of holly and came awassailing and we were the three kings from the Orient, following yonder star. I knew every verse of "Good King Wenceslas" and I sent my servant treading home in my footsteps when he could follow me no longer.

My father bent a thick wire into a circle a yard across and tied pine branches round it, twisting them together into a bushy wreath which he hung on the screen door of the porch and ribboned with a piece of poppy-red satin he had kept from a fancy package the Christmas before. He hung mistletoe from a hook in the ceiling of the hall and caught my mother under it with a kiss that made her wonder for a moment what was going on, until she saw what was up there, and after that there was a lot of trapping and kissing as people passed underneath it.

In the evenings before bed there would be my father's reading of *The Christmas Carol*, so the house would be filled, too, with Marley's ghost and rattling chains and Tiny Tim. Old Ebenezer Scrooge sounded meaner even than last year in "Stave One" as my father boomed his words out in that deep bass voice of his, but Scrooge always got to sound pretty nice after the ghost of Christmas Future got through with him.

Excitement mounted. It snowed two feet and in the morning a white hump on the circular bird tray made the tray look like a huge wedding cake. The sun seemed to come up later and go down earlier as Christmas got nearer. There wasn't enough time in the days to really savor them properly. Shopping got hectic. In the hardware store we picked out presents for my father—a screwdriver, a hammer, a flashlight—and at the five-and-ten we selected powder puffs and combs and kitchen spoons for my mother. We made things in our rooms, our own Christmas cards with crayoned trees and stars, "Merry Christmas, Mummy," "Merry Christmas to Daddy." "Merry Christmas even to you, dear brother, whom I actually hate but Christmastime has softened my heart to such an extent that I will deign to express good wishes at this time and I even promise not to beat you up for a whole week."

Finally, it was Christmas Eve. At dinner everybody tried to pretend nothing was particularly special. But everything was. The food tasted more delicious, the air smelled fresher, sweeter; sounds came at a higher pitch; sights seemed sharper, colors richer. It was the same house we lived in all those other 364 evenings, the same rooms, the same furniture, the same stairs, the same people, and yet they seemed now some-. how different, transformed, as if we were dreaming a good dream over again, knowing all the scenes, trying to make the dream stretch out as long as possible.

After supper we took our baths, soaking and lathering and getting ourselves really clean for Christmas day. We drew Christmas stars with our fingers on the steamed bathroom window, dried ourselves, got into pajamas and wrappers and slippers, and we crawled under our beds for the secret hoard of presents we had been storing up and wrapping all week. We carried them down to the living room and placed them under the tree in different piles. Then we were back upstairs to find the biggest stocking in the house. My sister owned knee socks. That wasn't fair, so my brother and I raided our father's high chest of drawers and came away with a couple of giant ski socks. With safety pins we clamped the ankle of each sock onto the black wire-mesh screen in front of the fireplace. My father hung a small one for himself, and my mother suggested that she should use one of her silk stockings, which would hold the most loot of all, but she ended up with a little sock of my father's she had knit herself and then shrunk by mistake in the wash. We also put one up for our baby sister and one for Hundy, pulling him in by the collar and letting him sniff his stocking that would have chewy dog candy in it the next morning.

Now we scooted into the kitchen and climbed up to the

cupboard and got graham crackers and Saltines and we poured a big glass of milk and placed it all on a little table set up beside the fireplace. We got paper and pencil and wrote a note to Santa saying we hoped he would like this little snack, and asked him to leave some nice things and to give our love to Mrs. Claus when he got back to the North Pole. My father sat in his big stuffed chair and we perched around him like brownies, on the arms, on the back, Nancy squashed down in the seat beside him as he read *The Night Before Christmas* to us. The tree showered the back of the living room with dancing colors and the star on top with its frizz of tinsel and its sparkling points seemed to shine so brightly that it could have been, yes, it was, the star of Bethlehem itself.

We said good-night and Merry Christmas a thousand times and finally we were in our beds, certain that it would be absolutely impossible to fall asleep at all that night, that we'd just lie there thinking, waiting, listening, hearts going like mad all night long, until morning. Snow beat against the windowpane. I threw the window up and felt the cold against my face. The radiator hissed. Through the blackness came sounds of journeys up and down the attic steps. Wise Men danced in my head on that silent, holy night, that cold winter's night that was so deep, that midnight clear, where the world in solemn stillness lay. Mangers danced there, too, and reindeer, a little old driver, Marley's ghost, a flying sleigh, dash away, angels, snow-howl, Our Lord Emmanuel, stockings and chimneys, glory to the newborn King, footfalls on the roof, gold and frankincense and myrrh, and radiant beams and mystery.

The blocks of white light on the snow below my window finally were extinguished as the kitchen lights were put out. More journeys to the attic by my mother. A prayer for all the lame and poor. The snow building up in a little pile on the window sill. Blanket snuggle. Never get to sleep. Never. Never all that night long. Turn over. Try to block up the mind. Never.

And then all of a sudden it was Christmas morning. I could hardly believe it. When I opened my eyes, my brother was standing over me, peering down, his face close to mine, close enough to make sure I'd wake up. It was just starting to get light outside.

"What's the matter with you?" he asked. "It's Christmas. The day's practically over."

He'd been up since four or something, plodding around breathing on people's faces, trying to get the day started. He didn't have to try too hard with me. We shook my sister up, too, and the three of us formed an instant army outside my mother's and father's bedroom. We cracked the door, we saw something stir under the heap of blankets—a sleepy-seed face, mussed hair, the smell of sleep. We rushed in, "Merry Christmas!" There followed a bit of moaning and tossing on my father's part—trying to suck a moment's more sleep out of the pillow   but before long we had them up and slippered and bathrobed, and nobody was even allowed to wash his face or brush his teeth or anything like that, it was right to the head of the stairs where the parade formed up.

We jostled for position, although the order of descent was prearranged by height—Edith first, held by Ken, then Yo-Yo, me, Nancy, my mother, Sophie, right on up to my father in the rear. Nancy broke ranks and went halfway down the stairs, straddled the banister, slid over and lowered herself to the piano bench below. She tested a note or two, looked up to see if we were all ready. We were—and then some. So she started to play. "The first Noel, the angels did say." To the plinking notes we marched slowly down the thin line of stairs, our left hands sliding along the smoothness of the banister, until we got to the bottom step from which we could see into the living room for the first time, and at that point the parade turned to bedlam, all order ceased, my sister gave up the playing and leaped from the piano bench to follow our mad rush into the living room to face Christmas.

There it was. We stopped, aghast. It seemed a different room from the night before. It seemed a room of dark and burnished gold. It quivered. Was the rug the old usual rug? Were the curtains the curtains from the night before? Were the couches and the chairs couches and chairs we'd ever seen? Or had wings during the night flown magic raiment in?

The first sight was always the fireplace. The screen on which the stockings were hung had been swung aside as if to clear a path right out of the fireplace itself for a fat jolly old elf. Ashes from the hearth were strewn all over the place —somebody in a hurry had booted around there. And, of course, there were some ash footprints made on the brown carpet, big white ash footprints that led from the fireplace to the little table where we had left the milk and cookies. That was the second sight we always saw—the empty glass with the coating of milk still left on the inside and the crackers and cookies gone, except for some very obvious big crumbs on the table. There was the note we had left, and below our signatures there was a note back to us, scrawled in some strange wriggly North Pole handwriting: "Oh, that milk and those cookies were so good," the note said in its big red letters as we grabbed it up and read it aloud. "Mrs. Claus always sends a whole box of cookies with me for my long ride Christmas Eve, but this year Vixen and Prancer got into them while I was down the Jenks' chimney, and so I was feeling very hungry indeed and was pleased to find these fine grahams and Saltines as well as this delicious cow's milk. It certainly beats polar bear milk. I hope Dasher didn't wake you up on the roof. He tripped a bit when he was landing and his hoofs made some noise on the shingles. Clean your chimney—my nice red suit is getting all black. Merry Christmas. Love, Santa."

That's the kind of thing it would say, and reading it aloud we tried to remember if we had heard Dasher trip on the shingles in the middle of the night, or had it been sighing old beams in the attic, or creaking trees or lurching snow or crying wind or flashing, silver dreams.

Then there were the stockings—swollen, heaving, bulging in a hundred places, things sticking out the top, making the leg fat and square, pushing the heel all out of shape, making the toe huge and round. We grabbed them off their hanging places and began to open.

It was like a magic stocking—how could so much good stuff get inside and keep coming out with every thrust of the hand? A puzzle. A jackknife. A deck of cards. Chocolate cigarettes. A magnifying glass. Pencils, pen, ink, crayons, a silver dollar, a Mickey Mouse wristwatch. Nickel pencil sharpener, dice, maple sugar man, camper's handkerchief, a pedometer. Fish line, hooks, hockey puck, dime bank, belt buckle, new toy soldiers, bicycle horn, and in the toe, at the very end of the toe of the stocking, always a shiny orange tangerine.

Bicycle horn! Who had a bicycle? And then, not a moment before, we dared really look at the back living room where the tree stood. Maybe we had stolen a single look before and seen the big things standing there set up in front of the gleaming tree, but we'd tried to shut our eyes to them, our minds, as we read Santa's letter and opened the stockings. My father was standing beside the tree now in his bathrobe and day-old beard, smiling, trying to guide each one of us to the big present that was ours and not let us leap on something that we thought was ours only to read the card and find it wasn't. In front of his desk, supported by its kickstand, its handlebars gleaming, its rubber hand-grips just waiting to be gripped by a couple of hands, its red body, its black pedals, its chain, its spokes, its fenders, its balloon tires puffing and waiting for weight, its leather seat just calling for a ride—calling for *me*—was the most beautiful, flashy, fire-engine red, professional, shiny-spoked, whizz-bang, chrome-plated bicycle ever assembled by man or beast. When I had looked up from the stocking and got my first glimpse of it in the back room, my eyes had gone straight for my father's, and they had told me, yes, it was mine, and so now I was across the room and I leaped upon its saddle with all my might and would have toppled over to disaster had he not been there to catch and steady.

Those same guiding eyes had sent my brother to a remarkable machine in the middle of the rug and he was now squatting over it, touching the buttons, working its joystick back and forth and activating the works so that the Lionel Remote Control Airplane was roaring into flight. It was an airplane about a foot long with four windows on each side of the body, a single wing, a rubber propeller that whirred, and a long, thin light aluminum piece of tubing which attached its fuselage to the top of a pyramid-peaked tower. On the rug, around the pylon tower, was a circular metal runway with the names of nine different cities for landing— Los Angeles, Dallas, Atlanta, Washington, Philadelphia, New York, Boston, Cleveland and Chicago. Working the joystick and the throttle from the control base, my brother was taking off from Dallas, spinning around the tower, gaining speed, cutting the motor and gliding for a while, revving up again, suddenly doing a backflip or a side-slip or a tailspin, climbing, doing a roll as if he'd been stunt flying for centuries, now putting her in a nose dive straight for Boston and pulling her out at the last minute, shooting her aloft again, circling the control tower, the plane filling up the air of the living room, making the rest of us stand in the corners in awe, marveling at the sight and the whir and the stunts, wanting desperately to get a turn at the controls, watching with admiration as my brother brought her in for a perfect landing in New York.

My sister was swooning over her skis. They were standing up against the bookshelves, their tips right against Sandburg, shiny and red, with bindings dangling off them, and in the bindings, strapped onto the skis, were brand-new beautiful ski boots with red leather laces and shiny metal toe clamps.

"Oh, Daddy, oh, Mummy," she was sighing, showing definite signs of hysteria, "I can't believe it. They're so beautiful. They're the most beautiful skis I ever saw. And all I wanted, all I wanted in the whole, wide world. How did you ever know? How did you ever guess?"

How? I'll tell you. She'd hardly talked about anything else for the last month, ever since the first snow. All her friends had skis and she didn't and the hints came thick and fast with everything from widely advertised letters to Santa burned up the chimney to sad, well-placed remarks like "Joyce and Kathy went skiing today and they said it was really fun."

Of course, I never made any hints at all about anything like a bicycle, unless you think riding around pathetically with a stick between my legs for a horse was a hint, or sighing whenever my mother and I passed the bicycle exhibit in Sears & Roebuck's Christmas window. And obviously nobody in the whole family knew my brother was absolutely nutty, crazed, out of his mind, bo-bo, blowing his cork that year over airplanes.

Well, so we all got what we wanted. And if it wasn't the bicycle year for me, it was the castle year—a gray, wood fortress of a British castle armied with fifty tiny, perfectly uniformed, rifled-and-ready-for-action British toy soldiers, some of them Scotch with kilts and one with a bass drum and one with bagpipes. Or it was the workbench year, a wooden workbench with all my own tools—hammer, saw, chisels, screwdriver, plane, sandpaper, nails, drill with half a dozen bits, and a pile of lumber. Or it was the chemistry set year, a stand-up Gilbert box that opened into three sections of shelves and compartments, filled with all the delights and mysteries of science—little labeled jars of powdered chemicals, and potent liquids of various colors and viscosities, test tubes, clamps, holders, a Bunsen burner, mortar and pestle, measuring spoon, asbestos webbing, stand, vial, microscope, glass slides, the works—everything needed to do anything except make an explosion, which was actually the only thing I really wanted to do with all that stuff.

After the big unwrapped presents, there were heaps of boxes and packages and beribboned things under the tree, lying on the big low branches, hanging off the high branches. The whole business of opening took hours because only one present was attended to at a time, the opener reading the card first and wondering what was inside from the feel and the weight and the shape and the size and everybody else standing around helping wonder, the opener shaking it and ripping off the ribbon and the reindeer Christmas paper my mother had stayed up until four A.M. putting on. Off it came in a swish, a crumple, off the top of the box, off tissue paper —and there was just the sweater you needed, just the neat pair of slippers, just the most neebeejo leather jacket or foot-ball pump or pair of skates or disguise kit with tins of grease paint, an assortment of mustaches, rubber noses, ears that hooked on with elastics, eyebrows and fright wigs. Or there were games in cardboard boxes, games with mazes and maps and men to jump with, games with dice and with little black cups to shake the dice in.

After about two hours of giving and receiving, of opening and exclaiming, of kissing thank you and trying out or trying on and thanking again and hugging, my father would suggest some breakfast and he would lead the way to the dining room —the very spot Sophie had been trying to lure us to with smells of steaming cocoa and smoking cornbread. Breakfast on Christmas morning was always a rush because our second Christmas was coming up at noon thirty miles away in New York City and there just wasn't any time for comfortable, slow eating. Then, too, the telephone had started ringing, and it was my father's brother up on his farm in New Hampshire calling to say Merry Christmas; and then it was one of his Massachusetts sisters, then the other—for we wouldn't be seeing any of his family that day; and then it was my mother's father and mother, whom we would be seeing—it was their house we were going to—but neither of them could wait until noon to say Merry Christmas and was everybody well and hurry up and come and Merry, Merry Christmas again.

It was a tug leaving our presents there in the living room, each person's in a special pile—on a chair or in a corner or underneath a table—leaving them and going upstairs and getting dressed. My father usually had to do some snow digging to get the car out of the garage, and Nancy brushed her hair a thousand strokes and kept everybody waiting, and my mother made a pile of packages in the hall that we were going to take with us to the city, and I would be all slicked up in my blue suit and brand-new tie getting a last lick at my bike with the stand down so I could pedal it sixty miles an hour with the tire not touching the rug, and my brother just wouldn't leave that airplane to eat any oatmeal or comb his hair or do anything right. Finally there was a lot of horn blowing and rushing and picking out the couple of small-enough-to-carry-in-your-pockets presents you wanted to take on the trip. Then we all were in the car, Sophie and Yo-Yo ready to be dropped at the station so they could take trains to their homes, all of us waving good-by to our house with Hundy locked inside eating his special dog candy. We headed down the frosty hill, cutting the first tracks in the Christmas Eve snow as we curved down the long drive, spotted three deer nibbling bark off a tree beside the road, did the hairpin turns with a skid that made my mother scream for some caution in the driving. In the back seat we children were beginning to fight already over who got how much lap robe as the car edged out past the mailbox onto the main road which had been plowed clean, scraped, salted and sanded just for us to set sail for our second Christmas.

It was a long drive on back roads, then routes with red lights every few blocks, then highways, bridges, the Holland Tunnel—finally the city and my grandparents' house. We were always late, but it didn't matter. On the last mile my mother had her comb out, working over our heads, getting us to spit on a handkerchief so she could scrub away the smudges of Christmas candy from the corners of our lips.

There were the uncles and the men cousins on the sidewalk in their blue suits and holiday smiles, guiding families in as different cars arrived and parked and disgorged their loads of packages and people. Everybody was gathered in the halls on the first and second floors of the five-story house. The curtained glass doors to the parlor were closed. Occasionally the door would be cracked for a newly arrived father to smuggle in his armful of packages. If you could squeeze up the stairs past all those your-own-size cousins in their velvet dresses and their little white socks and patent leather shoes, if you could get past all those kisses and those handshakes and slaps on shoulders and the latest remarks about your growth from all those aunts and uncles and old cousins in lace dresses, and from imposters who were just always there for some reason or other, maybe you could find my grandfather and grandmother.

She would be wearing something green, she never wore any other color in her life, and she would be wearing a soft, floppy kind of hat because she'd been to church but she'd keep it on all day, and she would be truly happy to see you and her hands would flutter over your hair to comb it with her fingers even though her daughter had done the job in the car a few moments before.

My grandfather would shake hands and say, "Hello, Scout," and laugh with the delight of seeing me. "Hi, Gamps," I would say and my grandfather would look right into my eyes and there was something special between us, and I knew why so many people gathered at this house, drove so many miles on Christmas day to get there, but not only on Christmas day, on any gathering day—on birthdays and anniversaries, before weddings, on Easter, on Thanksgiving—and much, much later on in my life, many years later, at the funerals, when they started to come in my family.

So everybody was finally there and the hubbub was tremendous up and down the stairs, but my grandfather called for quiet, and suddenly there was quiet, and in the hush the parlor doors were opened and a gasp went up at the first sight of what was behind them—another tree, another pile of presents, packages and boxes and ribbons and gold and silver paper, reds and greens, almost filling the parlor along with the grand piano, the couches, the regal chairs, the fireplace with its pair of sitting white china cats guarding each side of the hearth. What a flurry of opening and holding up and thanking—but much more orderly here than at home, with ribbon being carefully rolled up and wrapping paper folded and boxes carried downstairs by the neat, orderly men cousins so there was never any mess, never any wild confusion or refuse, any junk-heap look to the place that characterized the Christmas morning we'd had a few hours before on the hill.

The presents were much more sensible here, too. Nothing like a disguise kit or a chemistry set—all that kind of good stuff had been given at individual homes earlier. Now the boxes we got at my grandparents' house were filled with new clothes, or other useful things, and older people were receiving ornaments and jewelry, and there were envelopes hanging on the tree for my grandfather's nine grandchildren, each with a crisp mint-new one-dollar bill inside, an oval hole scooped out of the envelope so you could see George Washington's face staring out at you.

When we had all been glutted with presents and given our own to everybody, something out of clay we had made at school and glazed for my grandmother, a paperweight or a pen-and-ink set or some golf tees or a magnifying glass for my grandfather—then the food started. Across the hall in the dining room, my father took up the carving equipment at one sideboard, my uncle at another, and, after a lot of knife wielding against the bone-handled sharpeners, both of them began dissecting equally luscious looking, perfectly browned twenty-pound twin turkeys.

We heaped our plates with white meat and marshmallow-topped sweet potatoes, with the creamed onions and fresh string beans, with cranberry jelly and rolls and butter and ice cream and chocolate and butterscotch sauces and pies and cakes with white and orange icings, with mints and striped Christmas candies. We stuffed our mouths and when no more would go in, we filled our pockets, too.

After the dinner, even though my grandmother disapproved, some of the men had the courage to smoke. An old uncle lit up a big cigar, a younger one tried a cigarette from a flat silver hip box, my father stuffed his pipe, struck a kitchen match on the seat of his pants and sent blue wreaths up to mist the ceiling air. My grandfather made a *tut-tut* noise with his tongue as he watched all this evil going on. My grandmother smiled through it all—but just let a female try lighting up and see what happened!

My own-age cousins and my sister and brother were up

on the fifth floor now, playing a game of tag, dropping water bombs down the stairwell, all the way down five floors, down toward an imposter's head. My father was getting angry about leaving. He could not pry my mother loose. He was tired from the day and his smile was giving out.

Finally the good-bys—it was growing dark already. The packing up of boxes in the trunk of the car, the final thanks, kisses again for the older people, a good kick in the shins for one of my cousins, my mother lingering, talking, lingering, talking, not being able to tear herself away, my father honking the horn for her, roaring the engine for her, the three of us older ones in the back seat struggling for the lap robe, Edith snuggling in the front. Then with a whole bunch of waves we were off, waving out the back window until the car finally turned a corner and we were out of sight, on our way home.

After we'd got through the tunnel, it was black night and sleet had started to fall and my father drove slowly, hunched way up over the steering wheel with his face close to the windshield, keeping the glass clear by rubbing circles with his hand, trying hard not to skid on the slippery highway. I had a window seat and began my annual Christmas-night game to see how many lighted trees I could count on the way home. They gleamed from the windows of the houses we passed, from the front yards, little ones, middle-sized ones, huge ones, pyramids of lights, some many-colored, some just white, some blinking, some with silver stars, some close by, some far in the distance. One hundred was easy to reach—two hundred, three hundred. My brother at the other window had started counting, too, but halfway home he was asleep and my sister and I edged the blanket off him so we'd have more for ourselves.

The windshield wipers scraped their beat against the sleet. I counted on and on into the night. Four hundred! We had come off the highway, along all the back roads, and we were in our own town again, circling its square. The big lighted tree in the middle of the square was four hundred and sixteen. We headed out, along our route, and finally, craning over the front seat, searching through the third-of-a-pie opening the wiper kept on the windshield, I spied our mailbox. My father slowed down, raced the motor a bit, turned up the drive and gave it all it had for the hill. We skidded, scraped, moaned, veered, slid, ground away, almost stopped, whirred our wheels, shot forward, chains getting a good grip, slid again, made the hairpin turns—up, up—and there were the lights of our house, left on that morning to welcome us home.

We crunched to a stop in the crusty snow. Everybody was fighting sleep, everybody but Edith and my brother. My father carried them in first, then came back for the presents in the trunk of the car. I staggered through the snow, kicked it off my boots on the front porch, felt the warm blast of the hallway, patted Hundy, went into the living room to check over my bike and give it a few pedals, waded back through the sea of paper and tissue and boxes which still filled the living room and which my father would start cleaning up after he'd put the car away in the garage.

I could hardly make the stairs. I measured them with my new pedometer but they didn't register any part of a mile. My mother was saying what a wonderful Christmas it had been to my sister and kissing her good-night. The dream was almost ended, but I knew I would dream it again all the years of my life whenever Christmas came. From bed I heard my father's footsteps on the stairs and I waited for him to come to say good-night, before drowning deep in Christmas sleep.

Thirty years or more ago all that took place, and now it is another Christmas. I am the father instead of the child, I am forty, I have recently returned from the hospital, I am supposed to take it easy. I help pick out the Christmas tree but I let Peter and Philip and Jean and Sandra do the trimming while I watch from the couch. They skate on the black ice of our pond and I watch from the window. They shop, coming and going, hiding their secret acquisitions from me as they pass my study. The biggest exertion I am allowed is putting three-year-old Sarah up on my shoulders so she can try to hang the star. She can't quite do it, so Sandra gets to do it another year. I am treated with kid gloves, like an invalid. I feel fine, though. But I am wondering at this Christmas just who is the father, who the child. Roles, the cycles of life, seem to be reversing. Just as my mother and father had done, Katharine and I have worked hard over the years to make Christmas special and wonderful for our children, to blaze the beauty and excitement of that day in their hearts forever. Now these same children are taking the initiative, they are picking up for me, they are making sure all the old traditions are kept alive. This Christmas, for the first time, is not for them. It is for me, from them.

On Christmas morning, using finger blinders, the children somehow get their stockings out of the living room without seeing anything else in there, and they bring them, as they always have done, into our bedroom for the opening. "Merry Christmas" is being thrown all around and Sarah is getting hugged by everyone and the seven of us sit cross-legged on the bed with the five bulging stockings. Suddenly, from behind a back, there is a sixth stocking—bigger even than the others—presented to Katharine and me by Peter and Sandra. In it is an electric carving knife, two windshield ice-scrapers, a tiny thermometer with a magnet on its back, some rubber house flies, disappearing ink, a hand buzzer, a wood plane, plus fake cigarettes with red spangled tips which shoot out dust smoke when you blow through them—just the ticket for Daddy, who has been told a few weeks before he can never smoke again.

After the stockings, we line up by ages and march into

the living room and there it is all over again—the tree with its heavy smell of pine, the gleaming star, the clutter of ash tracks, the crumbs and empty milk glass, the cries of happiness as dreams come true. It is a very special Christmas morning for me, for I am much aware of being alive, very happy about that, very grateful. That is enough of a present, as I stand in the living room of my house, with my children all about me, my wife's hand in mine. But they refuse to let that be enough. They've ganged up on me. They make me pick out a place to pile my presents and I choose the pearl-gray velvet wing chair in a corner of the room. Everybody in the family knows my craving for bottles and jars and pots, and so, when Sandra hands me a long, flat, carefully wrapped and ribboned box, I hug her with pleasure for the set of beautiful colored spice jars inside.

Jean has been making herself scarce the days before Christmas and now I find out why as I open her package and discover a beautiful long heavy green and yellow scarf she has knitted for me. Another hug for joy! Now Peter hands me a large box with a note Scotch-taped to the outside. "Merry Christmas, Daddy. Here's an old timer back for a second time." I open up and there is an old heavy parka of mine that I had worn to death over the winters until the zipper had broken and the buttons had popped off and the green khaki material had worn at the cuffs and the neck so that the stuffing had started to come out—my favorite coat in the whole world that I couldn't possibly part with but couldn't wear any more either. And here it is, suddenly completely refurbished—new zipper, buttons, and all the holes patched.

Finally, huge, seventeen-year-old shaggy-haired Philip hands me a book. It is a thin book, bound in cloth with bright colored stripes of different widths running across it. Its pages are blank, except for the first eighteen. They have been written on in pencil. Page one says, PBK III to PBK Jr. Page two is titled "Dedication." It says: "With a few ideas inspired by you and written for you, this short book attempts to include some of the feelings and experiences together we've shared. Memories and dreams can be as real as experiences, even when they are poorly expressed. I hope to add to this book of visions, and to create many new memories for you. With a giant-sized portion of love (luckily not measured in calories or carbohydrates), I dedicate and present this book to you, my father."

I cannot read past there right then, but later, alone, I do. The sixteen other written-on pages contain eight poems and two descriptive stories. They are about skiing on Mt. Washington, winter trips our whole family have taken together to Puerto Rico, the tiny island off the coast of Maine that we bought last summer. The writing ends with "Three Memories," the last of which tells about riding big waves.

All the sea's anger is headed
this way
And growing taller and wider
and you hear someone say,
"Ride it backward—it's huge,
hold your breath, here it comes!"
And doing all that
and clenching your gums,
You feel yourself rising,
taken up in that madness
But the higher you go,
the greater your gladness
Until taller than palm tree
And arms stretched out straight
You are thrown down to the sand,
By a surge of ocean hate
And you feel yourself
Wrapped about somebody's legs
Who has been sent down there too
And who sees the mistakes
of trying to ride that wave
like any other,
So you're laughing together
And he is your father.

✵✵

Plane Crash

I HAD A LARGE COLLECTION OF TOY SOLDIERS AND I ADDED to it each Saturday by going to Woolworth's and buying another with my dime allowance. They stood about three inches high, and they weren't really all soldiers —there were cowboys and Indians and pirates and sailors and backwoodsmen and pilots and knights. I played with them under my bed where it was dark and people could sneak up on other people for a surprise attack.

Among all my tin men was a special one. He wore a brown World War I uniform, and he wasn't much to look at because half the paint had chipped off him, and the silver hard-hat he had once worn had broken off and got lost, showing the unpainted crown and leaving a slightly bald look to the top of the head. This soldier's features were nondescript—most of the face paint had been banged off, too, but you could tell that he was young and very strong and thin and had been good-looking in a rough way, and that he'd been around, knew the score. This was Slim Barry. I guess those scars, those signs of battle and hard living and knowledge of the world, were exactly why I chose him. Slim was always the leader, the hero, whether he was fighting pirates, or leading his men through the Northwest Passage, taking on a dozen Indians single-handed or blowing up the enemy ammunition supply on a mission so difficult it had taken him not only underneath the bed but across the dangerous open floor, crawling all the way on his belly, to beneath the bureau where he had to slip into the river and run the wild, white rapids before swimming a moat, scaling a wall, getting rid of scar-faced guards with deft, silent blows.

Slim Barry, of course, was me. In an instant I could transform myself into Slim and the world I created for him and stay there for hours. I was Slim, too, as soon as I could get out of doors alone and up into the woods. Slim fought a thousand fights, got cut up pretty bad, almost got beaten each time, but never did. I met my men under the Greenwood Tree which was a giant evergreen on the back road of the hill. We camped there, figured strategy, laid plans, practiced shooting. We set off from there on expeditions that took us for raids or surprise attacks all over the hill, but we always ended up back there, underneath the Greenwood Tree.

There was another huge evergreen on the back road of the hill that was my smoking tree because it had a good bed of old needles for lying on and round dry twigs that could be snapped off just the length and breadth of a cigarette. If he felt like smoking a cigarette or a cigar, Slim could go throw himself underneath the great spreading white pine and snap off what he wanted, tap it against the back of his hand, moisten one end slightly with the lips, scrape a tiny twig on the back of his pants for a light, take that first long drag, inhale, slowly blow the smoke out, watch it glide in a blue maze up into the green of the branches, tap the ashes now and start to lay plans for the next attack.

It was all attacks and fights and wars of one kind or another. My make-believe men and I had them in the woods, in the fields, in our hut we built against the stone wall, the wooden sides camouflaged with painted rocks. We had them in the dungeon of the old greenhouse where there were chains on the walls for hanging enemies up by the arms and racks for torturing spies.

I could slide into my Slim Barry world of racing, riding, charging, cloaks, masks, feats of daring, of slashing fists, fast-drawn pistols, gleaming sword play, strewn bodies—a world of high adventure and my own special brand of justice— and stay there for hours, not hearing any of the real sounds, not seeing any of the real sights, cocooned in my own kingdom until a real voice, hoarse from calling so long, finally got through to me that supper was ready.

It was a Saturday morning. The telephone woke up everybody in the house. It was only six thirty and no one got up and went downstairs to answer it for a long time, hoping that it would just stop, but it didn't, it kept on ringing, and finally my father did go down to see what was so urgent. The father of the family that lived on the top of the hill was calling. An Army plane carrying four men had disappeared somewhere in our county during the foggy night. Only half an hour ago one of the pilots, bleeding and barely alive, had crawled into the yard of the veterinarian who lived on the far side of our hill, a few miles off. All the vet had got out of the hysterical, injured man was that the plane had cracked up in high heavy trees and the other three men were still aboard and maybe alive. The direction from which the pilot had stumbled and crawled indicated he had come from somewhere on the back side of our hill. The National Guard had been called in to help on the search but they did not know the territory. Could we help guide them?

Could we! Slim was dressed and ready in a flash. He knew exactly where the crash must be. He would lead them right to the scene. He jogged alongside my father down the front drive to the bottom of the hill, then up the back road that climbed steeply toward the place where the vet lived. It was still raining and fog shrouded the treetops. There were trucks arriving and soldiers with boots.

Had any of us heard anything during the night? Any explosion? Anything at all? No!

What's down that ridge? Just woods and then two small ponds hooked together by a tiny brook, we call the bigger one pollywog pond because it's so full of them.

And what's up that ridge? Is it such thick growth a man couldn't crawl out of there?

"Why don't you bring in the bloodhounds?" Slim asked. All this talk and no action. So now Slim set off to find the crack-up. It must have grazed the tallest treetops, he figured, and that meant the right-hand side of the road. He split off from my father and the soldiers who had begun to beat the woods, calling back and forth to each other to keep in voice communication in the dense wet fog-forest, and he strode with confidence, knowing every turn, tree, rock of the hill, being in complete command of the situation. He pushed fern aside, branches, bent the trunks of sassafras and saplings to get past. The rain grew harder. Slim moved more boldly. His sneakers were soggy and streams of rain ran down his arms, his legs.

At first, while Slim was still in hearing range of the calling voices of the Guardsmen, he was as cool as he had been on any other mission—hadn't there been hundreds like this before? Why should this one be anything special? With good tracking, ingenious woodsmanship, Indian ears, and all the little tricks and instincts and subtleties of searching out and tracking down enemies Slim had learned over the long, hard years, surely finding a few men and a downed plane wouldn't be too difficult. He almost swaggered through the sharp brambles, exulting in the pain of the nettles, swinging aside branches with cavalier thrusts of the hands and arms and letting them snap back like catapults behind him.

But then, as he got deeper into the woods, and the voices of the soldiers began to recede into the distance, began to be muffled by the rain, not real voices at all any more, and the trees loomed so high overhead, and the forest was seeming to close in about him, the pace became slower, more cautious, the confidence began to shrink, courage to ebb.

Then I stopped dead. Somebody had spoken to me from very close by. It was a small, still voice. I did not know what it had said, but I knew it was a human voice calling to me from somewhere close by through the wet green. I stood transfixed, dizzy. For support I leaned my hand against the trunk of a tree. The bark felt soft, oily. I pulled my hand away and looked at it and it was red. I looked at the trunk and it was all red.

And then I heard the voice again—a muted, pleading "Help." The second sound gave me my bearings and I could tell now it was coming from somewhere above me. I forced myself to lift my head, raise my eyes. And there, almost directly above me, thirty feet above me, locked in a vice of torn, bent, severed, twisted trunk-tops and high branches, was an upside-down airplane, one wing torn off, propeller gone, a man hanging from one of the mutilated doors by straps. He hung face down, his arms all crooked and bent the wrong ways, his face all blood, a blotch of brains mashed into the bark, the blood dripping onto the trunk of the tree, the blood coming down the tree in a red lace all the way to the ground, the blood on his face broken only by the whiteness of his eyes which looked down at me with the most agonizing, pleading look that ever could possibly have been on the face of man, the lips moving in a black crack, the blurred word "help" sighing out of them once more.

I could not move. I could not answer him. I looked and looked into his eyes. My head began to nod. It seemed forever that our eyes were fixed upon each other, he way up there hardly able to speak, to move, but needing me, me way down below, on firm ground, unable to do anything for him.

Then, finally, I was able to force my eyes away from his, leave those white eyes, and I looked further, past him, and there was another body in the trees, this one not moving, hanging by the middle, dripping arms and legs groundward. It was then that I heard a low groan from somewhere on the ground, a groan so hoarse, so filled with pain, that I was frozen once again. Only my eyes moved. They searched through the low branches and dipping ferns for the source of this new unholy sound. If it came from the ground, that meant I could get to it, be of some help. All it would take was a few steps.

I could not do it. Instead I turned and fled. I smashed away from there, breaking branches in my run, whacking the wet branches out of my stricken way, quaking deep within me at the sight I ran from.

I heard myself calling some words with a voice that was not mine. Was there no one left in the woods but me and what I had just left behind? I broke into a clearing and there was a Guardsman. I threw up my arms to get his attention and pulled at his shirt and pointed. "There!" I finally was able to say. "There!" And again "There, it's there!"

The Guardsman turned and went running and in a moment a whistle blew and all the soldiers were coming through the trees and soon I could hear them calling to the man hanging up there to hold on, they'd be up to him fast. There were crackings of branches as trees were being climbed and there was a high scream of pain.

Where was my father? I had to find him. I kept running, looking. I fell over a downed tree and cut my shin on a rock. I felt blood through my pants leg. There was no pain and I got up and ran further down the woods until I saw my father standing beside a Guardsman on the road. I slowed up, approached them walking. I needed to be near him, touch him.

"There you are," he said. "I've been looking all over. Worried half to death. They found the plane. They said a boy found the plane."

He knew it was me. I just nodded.

The soldiers cordoned off the area, keeping us back out of the woods as they worked. A sergeant was talking over a short-wave radio in his truck, reporting the plane had been found, that two of the men were still alive and to get the ambulance down there fast and they'd need some heavy metal cutters and a blowtorch.

Even though I tried to hide it, my father saw how frightened I was. We watched the brown trucks with their canvas backs go and come, and police cars and the ambulance arrive. I started to tell him, but I could not even do that. Yet I knew that my father knew. He also knew what was done was done. He did not ask me any details. Instead he told me thank goodness there had been someone around who knew the hill as well as I did, that I was responsible for saving some lives.

I knew different. As we stood there beside the trucks in the rain, my father's hand on my shoulder, I listened to the sounds of rescue far back in the woods, the calls of the brave men who were high in the trees now, working their ways up to the plane itself, tying ropes, cutting straps, lowering the man to the ground. I wondered how his eyes looked to them. And in some instinctive way I knew the hill would never be quite the same for me ever again.

I did not want to stay at the scene. I could not go. Finally, before anybody was brought out on a stretcher, my father said we would just be in the way now. Slowly, silently, we walked home together in the rain, back up the hill.

The Big Idea

ONE NIGHT JUST BEFORE CHRISTMAS TWO YEARS
ago it snowed a foot, and in the morning my
son Philip got a big idea. He would build a snow
house—not just a little igloo, but a towering, stand-up castle,
a project that would take all day at least, a day of shoveling
and packing and hollowing out. It was cold, and he was
wearing my boots, and I did not go outside, but several
times during the day I stood at the window watching the
large boy and his growing mountain. Now, thinking back
to the flashes of inspiration my father and I shared, I wish
I had got another shovel out of the garage and joined him.
People with big ideas ought to have company.

Back in my childhood, a big idea never got worked out in
advance. It had to be thought up on the spur of the moment
and then done without preparation because preparation
meant thinking about it, and if two people ever thought
about a big idea very long, they wouldn't go through with
it. That was part of it. The other part was that the idea had
to be truly a giant, it had to be monumental.

My father and I would be standing on the front porch in the early morning, having a look at the snow together, and maybe it was the way the Empire State Building looked thirty miles away, a tiny black target in a white world, or the way the clean snow made us feel like pioneers. Whatever it was, a big idea suddenly hit. "What would you think about cross-country skiing?" he asked.

"Yes, yes, let's ski a long way," I answered. It was as simple as that. We skied all day, over hills and roads, crisscrossing valleys and pastures, twenty miles of skiing, arriving home in the dark, wet and exhausted and filled with elated talk.

Or it was a summer morning with steam coming off the ground, sweat already making my belt soggy, Hundy lying underneath the porch, too hot to come wag good morning. "Let's go to the beach," my father said.

"Let's," I answered.

He thought for a moment, leaned down, felt the calves of his legs, testing them. "Let's go," he said, "on bikes!"

So we pedaled ninety miles in ten hours and got to Mantoloking in the rain and took a swim in the ocean and we ate bad food in the only restaurant and slept in a rooming house. Slept? Laughed! Listened through the thin wall to a woman being too cross to her child. My father was outraged. He pretended he was an agent from the child welfare agency, pounding the wall for peace and decency. That set me off into fits of giggles. But it worked. We could hear the mother being much nicer to her child after that.

The last big idea we had together was the best of all. The man who had walked with us the summer before in the White Mountains wrote us a letter, completely unexpected. He had a summer job as a fire ranger on a peak in the Blue Hills Range of New Hampshire. It was in the middle of a game preserve, the letter said, with wild boar and everything. After we'd read the letter, I knew there was something coming. And there was. "Let's go tonight."

It was Friday evening, so we called up George right then. He sounded very excited and gave us some directions. My mother made sandwiches, and just as the light was fading we set off in Chowdog, and we drove all night long, three hundred miles, the last ten with me hanging out the window looking for the white boulder. I spotted it and we pulled off the road and George came out from behind the boulder and said hello. We shook hands all around, and he said I'd grown. George had a big revolver strapped around his middle and he slapped it a couple of times and mentioned something about the wild boar.

We started up the mountain, George leading the way, picking out the trail with one of those long-barreled flashlights. He said for us to keep our ears open for the boar. It took us three hours to get to the top. It was almost morning now and before going into the shack to sleep we sat for a while on the big rocks and watched the moon.

In the morning after our breakfast George wanted to

show us all the sights. He put on his gun and picked up a big pail and we set off for the water hole. It was down the mountain quite a ways, and while we were walking George told us that all the country around was one big-game preserve owned by a lot of millionaires who came up in airplanes and shot antelope and wild boar out of the plane windows. He said a wild boar had rushed him yesterday and he'd shot it dead just in time. We asked to see the body but he said it was too far off. When we got close to the water hole, he told us to be quiet, there'd probably be wild boar drinking there. He pulled out his gun. But when we got there, there weren't any wild boar, so we dunked our heads in the water to cool off and then we filled the pail and walked back to the shack.

After lunch it was time for George to play us some music. He had mounted four loudspeakers on the roof of the fire tower which stood on the tiptop of the mountain about a hundred yards away. The first record he put on was a Beethoven symphony and it almost deafened us. The music echoed back from other peaks miles away, making it seem as if there were orchestras playing all over the mountains. Afterwards, when we could hear each other again, George told us the farmers twenty miles away in the valley below could hear his music on a still night. One wrote asking him to play more often; it calmed the cows.

On the drive home my father and I talked about everything that had happened. And he told me about how he and his best friend at boarding school had first thought up the idea of big ideas, how once the two of them had skied twenty miles from his home all the way to the school on the first Sunday evening of a winter term, skiing through the gates to the school just as the annual candlelight service was ending, watching the boys spill out of the chapel with their lighted candles, a hand cupped around each flame, as they tried to run them back to their dorms without having them blown out by the winter night wind. And how once he and his roommate at college had been asked to a Boston debutante ball that was supposed to be a costume party and how he had come up with the big idea of going as plumbers. How my father had telephoned the hostess just at the time the dinner was supposed to start, informing her that the two of them were in Cohasset with their car broken down and please go ahead with the dinner without waiting for them. Then how, dressed as plumbers, they went through the back door of the house where the party was being held, proceeded into the pantry, and began making a very loud repair operation right next to the dining room where all the guests were seated, banging on pipes and talking in loud voices. Until the noise got so loud and bothersome the hostess had to apologize to her guests and finally had to leave them and come into the pantry to see what the blazes was going on.

I listened and we talked until it was dark, and then I climbed onto Chowdog's shelf, just behind the driver's seat, and we talked some more until I fell asleep.

There were no more big ideas that summer. The next winter my father hurt his knee and couldn't extend himself after that. It was just as well. I had met a girl whom I wanted to be with on weekends, and even if another big idea had struck, I think I would have turned it down.

✳✳

Fair Are the Meadows

MY FATHER SPENT THE LAST YEAR OF HIS LIFE fighting mightily to keep alive. He was crippled from a knee operation that had gone wrong. He could not bend that leg, and to walk he had to wear a heavy iron and leather brace and use a cane. In the beginning of the year he retired from his job in the city and began working full-time for our community hospital, which had been a large part of his life ever since he started raising money for it in the 1930's. But internal hemorrhages felled him and his insides boiled with trouble and pain as deadly uremic poisoning began to slip him from us. Soon he was on the second floor of the hospital as a patient more often than at his office desk downstairs.

In the late autumn of 1962 my father was in his upstairs bed at home. When one of us called to say we were coming to visit, he would struggle up, get somehow to the top of the stairs, sit on the top step holding the banister, then edge himself down each stair, one by one—it would take him half an hour to make the trip—so that he would be in his chair in the living room to greet us with a smile when we arrived.

Once, toward winter, I worked late in the city and then drove out unannounced after midnight to the hill. I found the front door locked, climbed through a window and lay down on a couch in the living room so that I could be there in the morning for a visit with him. Except for me, only my mother and father were in the house, and all night long I heard her getting up at his call, tending him. "Oh, my love. That's it, my sweet boy. It's all right, dearest. You're my sweet husband. My love."

I could not bear to hear it, could not help, could not intrude. I lay there on the couch all night without sleeping, trying to come to terms with the knowledge my father was really and truly dying. I would probably see him only a few times more. I wondered what there was to say between us that had not been said. Was there anything that I should know from him or anything that he should know from me? Had he ever been as strong and powerful as my childhood memories made him? Had he been the wonder man that everyone who knew him believed him to be? Was he really possessed with that combination of gentleness and strength, wisdom and wit, warmth and understanding, courage and integrity, that made him stand out head and shoulders above the crowd. Or was he as mortal as I was, made up of mistakes, omissions, self-deceit, doubts? Wasn't his very gullibility, the way his heart went out to so many people at the expense of his own time and success, wasn't that a failing? And wasn't it for lack of courage that, in his work, he had never struck out for the horizons? Was his love affair with life too simple? Square? Naïve?

The next morning when I went upstairs to see him he was trying to hobble his way into the bathroom. He went slowly, grabbing onto pieces of furniture for balance, fighting the pain in his leg and through his body, fighting in the same way he had fought through football practice and games forty years before. "Come on, Kunhardt," I overheard him calling himself by his last name just as his coach had done it back in college. "Let's go now. Don't give up! You mustn't! Get on with you! Go!"

Now, six years after his death, the contents of my father's desk spread before me, I see even more clearly that those distant last sad cries of struggle were echoes of a young man, already struggling, determined to succeed, never to count the cost. All his sixty-two years he went about living in such a simple, deliberate way. When there were things he thought he should learn, he learned them. When there was practice to be done, he practiced. For a summer vacation from Harvard, he wrote a list of accomplishments he expected of himself the next few months. They are in a black loose-leaf notebook, its edges touched now with white from mildew, taken from a drawer in his desk:

.   .   .

Things to do this summer.

ATHLETICS: To prepare for football.

1) Calisthenics every morning possible. Be sure to get this in. Make list to check off days. Have separate list for high knee-raising.

2) Boxing twice a week at least and more if possible.

3) Passing football. This must be done regularly and for good stretches as absolute accuracy must be gained by the end of August. Three times a week at least.

4) A run in the early morning is good if it can be gotten in. Be sure not to lose weight by it. It starts things well.

GENERAL:

1) Keep up with tennis as much as possible.

2) See if some single sculling can not be gotten in.

3) Try and get in some pistol shooting.

READING:

1) *Aids to Reflection,* study well.

2) *Life of Roosevelt.*

3) *Bryce's History.*

4) Tennyson

5) Milton

6) German

7) French—put down books read.

. . .

The sparks of this earnestness were in him from his early childhood, but the boarding school he went to helped kindle them. Up until his eleventh year his teaching had been tutoring doled out by governesses in the big house in North Andover, Massachusetts. But one Sunday his father went to church, heard a guest preacher who was the founder and headmaster of an Episcopal boarding school for boys twenty miles away, was so impressed with the young rector's fiery, virile style, and also by the hardy fact that he had ridden his horse the whole twenty miles that morning just to preach at that service, that he asked him back to Sunday dinner. By afternoon both my father and his brother had been enrolled in Groton School.

For my father, at eleven, the wrench away from home was a hard one. His first letter to his mother mentions his older brother, Jack, and tries to disguise his homesickness.

"Dear Mush,

"I hope you are having a good time. I wish I was home very much and with you, but I am not having such a very bad time. Sunday afternoon we went out for a bicycle ride and got a lot of nuts. Monday we studied and in the afternoon I looked for Jack but did not find him. Today we studied and in the afternoon I looked for Jack but did not find him. I am having a touch of homesickness. I would love to write more than twice a week because you seem to do everything the same every day here. With love to baby and take as much yourself."

One of the things that delighted my father over his years at school was a secret hut he and four of his best friends built and maintained. It was in the woods a few miles from the campus, a place from which they could watch birds and feed them. Birds had always been his friends—as a child he wandered through the woods putting pieces of string in the bushes for them to help build their nests. The hut was perched on a small level place in the side of a hill which had rocky girdles bound about it. It was made of oak and maple beams, covered on the sides with pine boughs and juniper. Built against a rock ten or twelve feet high, it was called Utah, the scrambled letters of "a hut."

Even though it was off-bounds, the five of them approached the Rector and got his special permission for Utah. Two or three times a week they would sneak away from their classmates and run or ski or snowshoe over to their secret hut to do some woodwork or put more feed out for the birds. They used Utah until their graduation in 1919, but for two years—their eighth and ninth grades—they kept a Utah diary which tells the simple story of close friendships, love of nature, pleasure from high, hard exertion. My father wrote many of the entries.

The first—a Sunday: "Chief occupation was making improvements on Utah. P. discovered a partridge's roosting tree. R. found a skunk's hole. After scattering seed we started for school. D. was on bounds. Saw fox and deer and skunk tracks."

Feb. 22: "Went over in twenty-two minutes which is the record for running."

May 16: "Did a lot of cementing. Killed numerous cater-pillar nests. B. stayed home with his brother who's going in the ambulance corps."

June 7: "Found Utah was well smashed. Pity the cow. Decided to rebuild."

Feb. 19: "Blowing like fury. Able to go nearly forty to fifty yards at a time by wind without taking more than a few strides. Signs of squirrels. Cleaned place of snow and put out seeds. Very hard to go against the wind coming home."

May 21: "Many birds around. The valley was echoing with their songs. The dogflower was in full bloom so we went down and got some."

My father's years at the school were happy ones. He worshiped in the Gothic chapel twice a day, singing in the choir the hymns that seemed to be becoming the basic themes of his life—"Fight the Good Fight," "Onward Christian Soldiers," "Fairest Lord Jesus" with my father's favorite stanza of that hymn: "Fair are the meadows, fairer still the woodlands." He studied hard. He made lifelong friends. His instinctive mirth was contagious. He played tackle on the football team, in the winter he wrestled and skated and skied, and when spring came, he rowed on the crew and at the same time played outfield on the baseball team, leaping out of his shell after a race and running up the long road from the river to the baseball diamond so he could get his letter in every sport. He was a traditionalist. He was sentimental forever after about his school and his teachers and his years there.

There followed four undergraduate years at Harvard and two more at the Harvard Business School, preparing himself to help run his father's woolen firm. During his first year at graduate school he met my mother—who was a year younger, from New York City, expensively educated, with a very special mind that was to be a constant enchantment to my father for the rest of his life. Soon they were engaged.

My father's father did not approve of such an early marriage. After all, he had invested a great deal of money to educate his son to work in his business. And that son had not proved himself yet. My grandfather thought the marriage plan was hasty, tried to forbid it, but my mother and her parents stood up to him, were firm about the wedding and its date, and finally my grandfather gave in.

For the first year of their marriage my mother and father lived in two fourth-story rooms in a brownstone on New York's East Eighty-second Street. Then Nancy was born and they moved out of the city to a little house at the foot of the hill. A year later I was born, and almost immediately this family of four packed up for a year in Scotland so that my father could study the theories behind cloth weaving and selling and come back better equipped to run the New York office of his father's business.

He worked at this new challenge with the same determination and zeal as he had read books and trained for football in the summers of his youth. Every week he wrote back home to his mother.

"Work is getting on very well with me. I am concentrating and am already outstripping the first-year men in my classes. I am getting to feel that there is no end of learning about design and color, and that my mind will be all confused by the welter of patterns, weaves and changes. But of course I know that before I get through I shall unify, classify and whip the whole lot into order in my mind, where they will be stored for future use. I do hope above all things that when I get home I shall show Dad that this trip has been decidedly worthwhile . . ."

The year abroad ended abruptly with sudden illness. We returned to the United States in the winter of 1929 and my father entered a Boston hospital and was operated upon, having a great cut made down and across the right side of his back and the kidney beneath tied off because it was supposed to have been poisoning his system. The operation almost killed him—and did help finally do the job, that lack of a second kidney, thirty-four years later.

At the same time the stock market crash had thrown the U.S. economy into frightened confusion and it was not long before my grandfather's woolen company, overextended because of expansion loans, was broken to bits. The crash wiped my grandfather out, ruined his health and led to his death six years later.

Now we had moved to another rented house, this one high on the hill, the house my father would live in for the rest of his life. When I was six I remember our whole family setting off from it to visit my father's parents in Massachusetts for a weekend. They were living now in their gatehouse where they had been forced to move when they could no longer afford to keep their big house going. I remember my grandfather confined to a chair and how bald he was and how nervous children made him. My sister remembers him popping out his glass eye into his hand, to make her gasp—the real one had been ruined long before by high blood pressure. I remember the stables and the steam off the horses' backs and the long scalloped gardens and the tiled swimming pool with circular steps descending into the shallow end, but most of all I remember a tension to the weekend, an air of finality.

In the beginning of June, 1935, my father went up to Massachusetts again—this time to see his father for the final time. There had always been a distance between them. His father did not know how to be naturally relaxed and affectionate. My father had always felt that his father had not helped him enough at the times he needed help, had ignored him while he was a boy, turned him over to governesses. Then, after he had grown up, his father had not immediately supported him in his plans for marriage, was not instinctively generous. But that was his father's way, his nature. All the years of hard work and severe German ancestry had created a certain kind of man—dark, formal, reserved, a country person, quick-tempered but forgiving, businesslike, with a capacity to love that was often slow and hard to activate.

Now my grandfather was bedridden, poor circulation had created gangrene in his feet, strokes had partially paralyzed him, and my father sat by him on the side of the bed and they talked about many things, business and family and memories. Afterwards, after he had got back home, he told my mother that he had looked into his father's eyes and could tell he was saying good-by. He could also see for the first time in those eyes, he said, how much his father really loved him. And there, sitting on the bed, my father had forgiven his father forevermore any harsh or unthinking or seemingly unloving things he might have done or said to him in his life.

It was a few days later. The telephone rang and my father took it standing up, listening, silent. My mother hushed us up the stairs, it was a terribly important moment, she told us, and she demanded complete silence. I watched from the top of the banister as my father heard the news of his father's death and spoke something and put down the phone and turned to my mother and said, "Dottie, he is dead." And he began to cry and my mother put her arms around him and he cried in great shaking sobs for a long time.

A year later my mother had a very bad case of bronchial pneumonia and was in the hospital six weeks. There were no antibiotics then and she had constant injections of morphine. My father came to the hospital before taking the train to the city each morning and he came again after work until bedtime. He never let her know how desperate he was. Always he was planning for the cottage at the New Jersey seaside that he would rent for August and he would join us for his two-week vacation and weekends. My mother was in a continuous drugged dream. In that dream she lived—and it was barely living—for my father's visits.

One afternoon he found her weeping, terribly upset. The nurse said her fever had shot up. For the first time she was allowed no visitors besides my father. But the minister of our Episcopal church had managed to slip into her room to pay a call on her even though he had been asked not to, and the sign on the door said "No Visitors." He had knelt and prayed a long prayer that my mother's life be spared and then he had seated himself and asked if her children had been christened. My mother was too ill to receive all this lightly. She was indignant, furious that her privacy had been violated. That night she told my father about it, and angrily he saw to it that from then on no member of the clergy was to casually drop in on a parishioner whose name he happened to spy on the hospital lists. A visit would take place only at the request of the patient.

The thirties were hard years for my father, as they were for so many people. He felt lucky to have gotten a job with another family firm that made woolens, but his salary was small, so my mother set out to supplement his income by writing children's books. She illustrated her nonsense tales herself and they were published and well received; over the years the money she made helped send us to the private schools they both thought were so important for us. But these were gay years, too, for my mother and father. They had many friends and I remember their dinner parties, me sneaking a look from the top of the stairs as laughter and talking and clinking of plates and glasses and smoke and singing filled the whole downstairs.

My father's troubles and frustrations at business are explained in this draft of a long letter to his employer, written in the late thirties. "I have been terribly unhappy for the last four and a half years. I have tried to conceal this and do my work cheerfully, hoping that it would increase in amount and importance. I have been unhappy because I have not had enough to do to keep myself constantly occupied, and to be a mental challenge. I have suggested this to you several times and you have assured me that things would work out all right and that my responsibility would increase. But it has not, and for the last year or so I have said nothing as it seemed to get me nowhere. I have always believed that a man to be worth his salt must put more into his work than he takes out . . . I feel a slacker, sitting around and doing little, and making my weekends and life at home my whole life. Two days since you have been away I have been really busy, so busy that all but my work was out of my mind, and when I returned home my wife wondered because I looked so rested and happy . . . There is such a thing as intellectual honesty. I am not being honest with you or myself and therefore I am forced to seek employment elsewhere."

I do not know whether or not that letter was ever sent, and my mother says she does not remember either, but if it was, my father must have been talked out of his decision, for he stayed on with that company, although he never gained a high position in it. He just was not aggressive in business, although he was so well trained for his profession. Something in him simply could not push himself forward. And his lack of success in business sickened him with depression.

The early 1940's were the only bad years my mother and father had together. Once she came upon him unexpectedly with a bottle of bourbon tipped up, just drinking straight from it, after a long, disappointing, hopeless day of work in New York. Those were the years when he lost hope, or lost his dream of business success, and he wondered whether whiskey could make him feel the hurt less. But the drinking phase ended as suddenly as it had begun. My father was not a drinker by nature, and when he found he could feel his troubles just as acutely when he drank as when he didn't, he stopped, and my mother and he were happy again.

One of the things I discovered in my father's desk that was of particular interest to me were files he kept on his four children. It was nice to come upon the one marked P and find a whole dossier on me, everything from report cards to height and weight records, letters, notes, clippings, even my first curls in an envelope.

First-grade report card: "Has tendency to reverse letters. Responds joyously to rhythms, to the point of rowdyism. Has improved in being able to take censure without resentment. Accomplishes daring feats on the apparatus. Has a tendency to be spectacular, with an eye to the populous, possibly because he is the youngest in the class and has had to work a little harder than the others."

Second grade: "Exuberant, joyous, has moments—probably of fatigue—when he weeps easily, usually gay and twinkly."

It was a very progressive school, started by my mother and father and a few other young couples who felt the lack of a good primary school around our town, and at first it was housed in a big empty mansion on top of our hill. I could run away from it easily and hide in my woods, which I did a few times when a teacher had been too strict and I was feeling sad for myself. Most of the time, though, that first school was fun because the courses were things like "how to live like an Indian," and we would spend a whole autumn or spring making a village of teepees in a field and constructing tomtoms and tomahawks and stirring up war paint and planting corn and doing Indian dances and learning Indian customs. One of my friends got a poor report card in this subject, which upset his mother badly until their maid got to the heart of the matter for her—"I don't believe Arthur is ever going to be an Indian, is he?"

By my tenth birthday, my mother's father—my New

York grandfather—was trying to get me to face the facts of life and be a man!

"It is hard for me to realize that you are ten years old," he wrote me. "There are so many happy years ahead of you if you make the most of every minute of every day in these wonderful times when you are young and are preparing to take your place in the world.

"When a fellow reaches ten years, he has lived about one seventh of the time which men call the span of life. This span of life is divided into decades or spaces of ten years each. The second decade, until you are twenty, is the study period, for if you prepare for college and then study to be a doctor or lawyer, or an engineer, or an architect, which means that you would be a professional man, this study period takes more than ten years, and you could not begin to earn your own living so soon in life. Yet you would earn a better living by being better prepared. You must have knowledge before you can pay your way in the world.

"So today you are nine and tomorrow you will be ten. How fortunate you are to be the oldest son in a family like yours where nothing but love is to be found. You have such a wonderful opportunity to become a useful member of society, to have friends, to be more that just a boy."

I guess I didn't pay much attention to that letter, and didn't want to be much more than a boy yet. Even so, by the fifth grade, my parents had decided I ought to be learning something more than Indians, so they put me into an all-boy private day school.

One of the items in my father's folder on me that provoked considerable parallel thinking between generations was a clipping from that school's newspaper. I was eleven at the time. "Our opponents carried to the seventeen," it read, "but then a pass was intercepted by"—guess who—"and by a beautiful piece of open field running, he carried the ball over for a score."

This particular feat of mine was witnessed by my father, who took the afternoon off from work to watch me play. It was the first year I'd ever played real eleven-man football with an actual uniform. I was the left end and had been blocked out of the play and had fallen back and suddenly the ball was floating toward me, off course from its expected receiver. I can still see that ball coming down, realizing I could take it, leaping, feeling the whack of the ball against my cheek and shoulder pads as it almost bounced away, grabbing it hard, mindlessly heading out across the field, then down and cutting back again, outrunning all those crimson jerseys across the white chalk of the goal line. On the way back up the field I sneaked a search for my father in the crowd on the sidelines. Had he made it out on time? I loped nonchalantly back up the field through the happy calls of my teammates, and then I saw him there in his business suit, cheering madly. Not wanting to seem overly proud about the run, I quickly looked away just as our eyes met.

In the autumn of 1940 I was twelve years old and packed off to Groton the same way my father had been thirty years before, with "½ gross clothes name tapes, a napkin ring, picture frame, small strong box, arctics, Bible, prayer book, hymnal, pair patent leather shoes, garters, collar buttons, blue Sunday suit, $5.00 in cash," and forty-five other required items that the printed announcement I found in my father's P. folder stipulated.

My first letter home was not very different from the ones my father had written back to his family so many autumns before.

"Dear Mum," the first one begins, "I am sitting in the big study hall writing you. So far I have had a wonderful time. I got some sneakers yesterday. I had a good day yesterday after you left. Write me soon and tell me how everyone is. Be sure to give my love to Edith and everyone else. Now chapel is starting so I will have to mail this after chapel. Well, I send you all the love in the world. With tons of love."

When my parents came up to visit me at school on a weekend, I would spot them way off and I would run as fast as I could and kiss them hello. Not many boys at the school kissed their fathers, I noticed, and so about my third year there, when my parents came up, I approached them slower, aware that I was being watched. I kissed my mother and then I turned to my father. He knew exactly what was going on in my mind and he waited for me to make the first move. When he saw it was not to be a hug or a kiss as it had always been before, when he saw it was to be a handshake, he smiled and put out his hand to meet mine. We did not kiss again until the last years of his life, when I would come to visit him on the hill, and then, some twenty years later, I took the initiative a second time and began kissing him on the cheek each time we met or parted.

Off in the woods behind the school my best friend and I built an against-the-rules underground hut. We dug a great square hole and covered it with planks, spread sod and leaves on top, leaving a little slide passageway for entrance, and that became our secret meeting place. We broke rules like mad, and I used to tell my father about our escapades and he would shake his head and say, "You'd better watch out, you'll be kicked out if you don't." But the episodes would amuse him, too—make him think back.

Now when my wife and I visit our two boys at Groton, they come right up to me and kiss me hello, they don't ever hesitate to think of a handshake instead. I wish I had been as brave or unconcerned or natural as they.

Both Philip and Peter seem to enjoy going over the old formal class and team portraits that hang on the walls of the school corridors and picking out the little faces of my father and my father's brother, and then going along the row of photographs, past World War I, past the twenties, past the Depression, into World War II years, and finding the faces of me and my brother, peeking out or clowning or posing or frowning or looking very serious, faces that change and grow in each case from small boy to young man.

When they come home for vacation, they just sit around for the first couple of days, loving to be home and not wanting to do anything special, wanting only to reacquaint themselves with their rooms and our house. They look at television and play with their sisters and rub the ears of their dogs. They don't say much at first, but after a while one might open up with some stories about the term that has just been concluded. I get nervous when I hear about their huts and all the rules they've broken.

One of them told me that on the night before the last graduation day he and a friend decided to de-charge the big bell on top of the schoolhouse, fix it so it couldn't ring, and then, because every event of that last day is signaled by that bell, havoc would reign. So at three in the morning they got up and put on all-black cat-burglar costumes they'd been assembling for weeks—even sneakers dyed black—and they lowered themselves out of their windows on ropes, sneaked across to the schoolhouse building, climbed stealthily up to its bell tower, hauled themselves right up to the bell itself, and by flashlight they took out the pin that holds the clapper on, pocketed the pin, and made the trip back to their dormitories.

"You're going to get kicked out of there. What's the matter with you? Are you mad?" I said.

He just answered matter of factly that I should have seen the riotous effects it had on graduation day. I told him he was a criminal, destroying other people's property, and he told me he left seventy-five cents in a little paper bag right alongside the clapper and a note saying the money was to pay for a new pin. So everything was fine.

Then he told me about his trips through the dangerous, off-bounds network of huge heating pipes that run underground from the school powerhouse to each of the buildings and coil up through the thick walls and ceilings to bring hot air to the corridors and rooms during the winter months. I groaned when he told me he almost fell down a thirty-foot chute and groaned again when he assured me it would have been certain death. But I couldn't get too annoyed when he told me that at the end of exploring the tunnels with a flashlight, he finally came upon a tiny ending room at the furthest reach of the pipes and on the wall he found my initials carved there, and underneath them, *1943*. Before leaving, he said, he added his initials alongside mine and a *1967*.

What else was in my father's desk? Evidence that he was a sentimental man, a man of order and habit. His yearly checkbooks, all packed away under the desk somewhere, show the tidy, exact way he kept his finances. He had a small trust fund left to him by his father's brother, and in many of the hard years the income he got from it made the difference. Every three months a check came from the trust and my father would enter it into his checkbook as a deposit, and then in the margin, each time over all those years, those decades, right up until his death, he wrote, "God bless Uncle Wheaton."

He was a man who believed that self-sacrifice and service to others shed grace upon one's life, and so he offered himself to our grade school and became its president, and to our town library and became its president, and to the community chest and became its president, and to the community hospital and became its president, and to the Harvard Club of New York and became its president. The piles of papers and reports and letters that record his work for those institutions and for his church as vestryman took up two long drawers in his filing cabinet beside his desk.

The forties were my boarding school and college years and in 1950 I married Katharine and left the hill for good. It was almost as if my father was making amends for his father, he supported me so fast and so completely in everything I chose to do. He backed my choice of a wife, loving her from the first instant he knew I loved her. He backed our marriage plans. He gave us every bit of financial help he could, and then some. We were living in California in the fifties, and if he got wind that one of us was sick, or that Katharine needed someone to help with the cleaning when we couldn't afford help, or that there was a chance we could fly back for a visit, a check would be in the next mail. Whenever I asked him for advice about my job, he gave it to me with great concern and thought, but it was always good, daring, vigorous advice.

A few more things in the desk: Lists of every book my father read each year from his college days on. Dozens upon dozens of books each year, because his first commuting rule was never to read past the front page of the newspaper, his second never to talk to anyone on the train. He'd read a book, and if he liked the author, he'd read steadily through all that author had ever written—all of Dickens, all of Dumas, Kipling, Stevenson, Hardy, Emerson, all of Sandburg, all ten volumes of Nicolay and Hay's *Life of Lincoln*. He also read fishing books and nature books and books of high adventure and the best novels of each year. Always the last entry, in late December, would be *The Christmas Carol*. When we children didn't want to hear it any more, he read it to himself.

And then, score upon score of carefully set-down, handwritten notes he wanted to keep: "Edith means the blessed / therefore everything that she should ask or care for / shall if good for her be granted."

Or quotes from poems or plays or essays he had particularly liked so many years ago when he was a young man, sentiments that he had decided to live by, to carry in his wallet, or keep in his desk, to come back to time and time again:

"There is no way to success in our art but to take off your coat, grind paint, and work like a digger on the railroad, all the day and every day"—EMERSON

"How low, how little are the proud"—GRAY

"Whosoever has lost heart in these times of disillusion, rouse your courage, hope on"—WAGNER

". . . loved him for his copious peacefulness and for the mountain landscape of his mind, with its darting lights and shadows"—VAN WYCK BROOKS

"Welcome, O brown October! Like a monk with a drinking horn, like a pilgrim in russet"—LONGFELLOW

"That was love, then—the going into a place apart of two souls, for whom even the dark avenue of death could hold no fear"—CONSTANCE HOLME

The last year of my father's life was suddenly upon us. No one was willing or had the courage to admit it at first, not even to the privacy of our own hearts. No one, that is, except my mother. But the doctor finally told us straight out. There was no hope. It would be a matter of months, then weeks, finally days.

Now, of course, there were no more morning cannonball sounds from our pool deep in the woods as my father made his dive, my mother on the front porch waiting for the watery thud, worrying that he was alone in that icy water, timing him the ten minutes it took him to reappear in his garden and start examining his flower beds. It was a year of doing things for the last time. But at least now, working for the hospital, he had finally found the kind of employment where his simple business philosophy worked—work as hard as you can and do the very best you can every day and things will come out right. All the big givers were his friends and he had been getting money from them for the hospital for years during evenings and on weekends. Now every potential donor, rich or poor, was his responsibility, and he labored over letters to send out, and studied medical bulletins and magazines so that he could know the latest treatments and could be persuasive about having a staff and methods equal to the hospital's bricks and towering glass.

It was a heart-rending summer for my mother. On June 25 her father died in his ninety-sixth year. My mother and father drove in to New York City together for the funeral in the same church where they had been married so many years before. Several months later, when the awful truth of her husband's death finally broke into my grandmother's mind, she had a massive stroke, which never allowed her to utter a sound from that day forth, or to move even her little finger, though tears sometimes rolled down her cheeks. So the sadnesses were mounting.

During that summer and fall the last times began to quicken for my father. He took a trip to see his brother Jack in Francestown, New Hampshire, my mother always at the wheel now. And he took with him the beautiful oil painting of the shepherd tending his flock that had hung in our dining room, one of his truly prized possessions, for he wanted his brother, who raises sheep, to have it. My father did not consult my mother about it, as he always consulted her on everything, he simply made the decision. It was his way of saying something final and loving to his brother.

His last fishing trip to his beloved Beaverkill could not have been more of a failure. Suddenly my father's blood pressure had shot up, the potassium in his kidney was high and no amount of pills in all the bottles he had with him helped. He was hobbled by the brace on his leg. He could not move without crutches, and it was out of the question that he could again stand in the water to fish, he would have to manage from the bank.

My mother carried one of the heavy straight chairs from the dining room of the clubhouse and put it in the car. She drove him to the place where the river flowed nearest to the road so he had only a few steps to go. My mother carried the chair to a spot he pointed out, a little way from the bank of the stream, and he sat in it. She handed him his rod and reel and box of flies and landing net that he knew perfectly well would never land anything again. And for a long time he chose the right fly and tied it on his line, looked up at the sky and the trees some distance behind him, and with a mighty effort, made his cast. The line rolled backward in a wavering loop through the air and the fly with its hook caught firmly in the branch of a tree. Neither of them said anything. Somehow my mother got the line down with quite a big piece of branch and leaves on its end. It took so long to get back into the car and drive up to the clubhouse that it was a little dark—and certainly dark in their hearts. In the morning when they started home my father devoured every flower and tree and glimpse of the Beaverkill with his eyes. He never said aloud good-by to anything, but that's what it was—good-by to another thing he loved.

On Christmas day, less than two weeks before his death, Katharine and I drove over to the hill. Somehow Dad had got himself down the stairs for a final time and he was sitting in his chair beside the fireplace. He gave each of us green and gold cards with checks inside, just like any normal Christmas. But the messages he had written on the cards in his still-firm, perfect script, were different. They were telling us good-by. "For my sweet daughter—May the Lord make his face to shine upon you." "For my sweet son—May the Lord reward you with every good thing of this life."

A few days after Christmas he was back in the hospital. My mother knew he would never see his hill again, his house. She wanted him to see the things he had lived with so long and loved so much a final time, and it was all she could do not to call out to him, "Look, look into the living room, at the fireplace, the china parrots on the mantel," as they carried him downstairs, past the living room door and outside to the ambulance.

January came, as it had for him now sixty-three times. He grew weaker by the day. Pain seeped through his body, consuming him. He could no longer move, could not raise his head off the pillow. He was dressed in a white hospital smock. The only possessions he had with him lay on his bedside table—his gold wristwatch, a second pair of glasses, his wallet. But he could not see even these. His vision had become blurred. My mother took my father's new little calendar notebook for the year 1963 and, for her own record, filled in the spaces for the four days he lived that year. Just a few words in each space, as he had done for decades.

TUESDAY, JANUARY 1: Moved from special care to fifth-floor private room, three nurses.

JANUARY 2: "Dottie darling, I'm afraid you won't have me much longer. I'm sinking down. I'm losing contact with the world. Hold me."

JANUARY 3: The doctor told me that he would give him no medicine to quiet his agony of mind, that no man should be denied the experience of death and have his personality taken away. Said he would live one week or ten days.

JANUARY 4: "Dottie, Dottie, I haven't much courage left."

On that afternoon, his last, my mother telephoned the Rector of St. Peter's Church, who was a close family friend as well as our minister. She remembered vividly thirty years before when a different minister had made that unasked-for visit to her during the time of her pneumonia. The rule that clergy could visit patients on request only still stood. Now that request was being made, for my father seemed to be very much worse though completely conscious, too conscious, and my mother wished that the suffering in his mind could be eased. Our rector said he would come over immediately, and in moments, dressed in the white flowing robes in which he conducted services, he was standing beside my father's bed, reading to him from the Bible. My mother had not mentioned to my father that he was coming and afterwards neither of them mentioned that he had been there. At the end he held my father's hand and said, "The Lord will help you. You know that, don't you, you know that he will help you." My father answered quietly, with that incredible dignity that seemed to invest him at the last, "He has already helped me."

There is no entry in the little diary for January 5, which is my brother's birthday. Ken was thirty-three years old that bright winter morning. My father had been so pleased to have another boy. And that boy was born in his image and he loved him so, it was a good morning for our father to go.

For the rest of that day, and the next and the next, we huddled together in our house on the hill. The days were not spent mourning. They were too filled with telephone calls to my father's closest friends and relatives, with the writing and the arrangements for the death notices, with the plans for the funeral services and the burial. Lists had to be made up, pallbearers asked, honorary ones invited, the service gone over with the minister, exactly the right psalms and prayers and hymns chosen. In my father's desk, in one of its drawers, I found his father's black, leather-bound prayer book. He must have taken it to his father's funeral and then put it away forever, for its marker still lay at page 324— "The Order for the Burial of the Dead." I read it through slowly, for the first time in my life really listening to each word. "I am the resurrection and the life, saith the Lord . . . For a thousand years in thy sight are but as yesterday, when it is past, and as a watch in the night . . . I will lift up mine eyes unto the hills; from whence cometh my help . . . My soul fleeth unto the Lord before the morning watch; I say, before the morning watch . . . I am the way, the truth, and the life; no man cometh unto the Father, but by me . . . Man, that is born of a woman, hath but a short time to live . . . earth to earth . . . I heard a voice from heaven . . ."

My mother and my brother and I visited the undertaker's display room and chose a heavy gray box with metal bar-handles running along either side. When my father was in it, my mother wanted to see him one final time. Before entering the dark, curtained room where he lay in the open coffin, she grasped my brother with her right arm, me with her left, and we marched in and looked at him. He had the bad waxy look of embalming. She knew he wasn't there any longer, she had already said good-by, she was just making sure his collar was straight, and his tie, as she had always checked them each morning before he left for work.

We went to the florist he had used for decades whenever he wanted to send some winter flowers to her, and we ordered a blanket of yellow roses to cover the coffin. My brother and I decided that at the end of the funeral service, his two sons and his two sons-in-law and his nephews would pick the box up and carry him down the long aisle and out of the church—no rolling devices, no stranger-men in black suits doing the final march.

The letters had begun to arrive, dozens at first, those dozens followed by hundreds upon hundreds over the next weeks. My mother read them first and then we passed them around. She read them slowly, thinking of the person who had done the writing, thinking back, studying the words that particular friend had chosen to use about her husband.

The letters to my mother I particularly liked were the ones that talked about her, too, and the quality of their partnership.

"From the moment of his marriage to you, his glorious enjoyment of life became a wonderland of delight. Aside from the daily enchantment you provided for him, you made him become what—wonderful though he would have been in any circumstances—he could never have been but for you, a creature of tremendous perception and delicacy of understanding which, added to his natural charm and vigor of mind, made him one of the rarest people on earth . . . nothing will ever fill in the great crater in your life. There is nothing now but to bear it . . ."

Even though written in the passion of loss, the truth shined through those letters. Would he have liked to know how many people felt so strongly about him? Would he have wanted to hear those trumpets sound? No, he would not have listened or believed it. That was part of his secret.

Over the next weeks I received many letters, too. The one I prize most, which says what I could not find the right thoughts and words to say then, came from one of my dearest friends who has mourned his father's death ever since he was seventeen.

". . . Yesterday, seeing your mother's superb dignity and

your own calm pride as you carried that heavy box under those yellow roses down the aisle, looking round that packed church at your family and all those friends, I remembered my father's funeral and realized again as I have been realizing for some time now that it is wasteful to mourn so long, that my father's love for me, as your father's for you, has left me able to take up cycles of my own and to start them in my children . . . So you and that kind man have done something to me. I pray him peace."

Yes, I pray him peace, too. That's what we all were trying to tell him as we thundered out Christian Soldiers in that packed cathedral, as we told him how fair were his meadows, fairer still his woodlands. That is what my brother and I were trying to tell him the afternoon before the funeral. It was a sunny, cold afternoon as we drove off the hill, through the town with its flags at half mast, to the towering Episcopal church. In its chapel our father lay in state. We were taking a sweetheart rose to put in his lapel. Whenever they were in bloom in his garden, he cut one and with the dew still on it he wore it to work in the buttonhole of his suit coat.

There was no one else in the church. Our footsteps echoed off the high stone walls and pillars. Stained-glass light sprinkled the marble floor. The smell was of shoes, kneeling pillows, church dust. My brother and I stood by the coffin, afraid to raise its lid. Finally one of us got the courage.

And there he was, sleeping in his best blue suit, too stern

a look for him, too still a face. He should have been wreathed in smiles, the crinkles coming off his eyes, his mouth filled with laughter. He should have been blowing smoke rings for us to stick our fingers through. He should have been making his little boy's face over the thoughts of our next big idea.

My brother and I fitted the rose into the buttonhole. Our hands trembled. I touched his chest, knocked it lightly twice with my knuckles. It was hard as iron. We straightened his tie for my mother. We kissed him good-by and wished him peace and closed the lid and went home to our empty hill.

Epilogue

I T IS SPRING ONCE MORE. ANOTHER CYCLE. A FLIGHT OF geese arrows north over our house. I have started going to work again. Soon my boys will be coming home from school for their summer vacations. They talk about working on a dairy farm. In June our sixth child will be born. In August the whole family will go to Maine.

I have already carried the two suitcases and the three cartons that hold the contents of my father's desk back down into the cellar and piled them in an out-of-the-way corner. The case with the boxes of color slides sits in a closet, awaiting my next trip to Massachusetts when I will take them back to my brother.

As for the desk, my mother gave it to my wife and me when she moved from the hill. The crack on its top has widened a little this year. Someday the desk will be owned by one of our children. And then it may begin again to hold a record of yet another life.

About the Author

PHILIP B. KUNHARDT, Jr., grew
up in Morristown, New Jersey.
After graduation from Princeton
in 1950, he went to work at *Life*
magazine, where he is now Assistant
Managing Editor. He is the co-
author of *Twenty Days* and lives
in Chappaqua, New York.